Volume Isn't a Strategy

A Credit Union Leader's Guide to Indirect Auto Lending

CU Risk Advisors

ISBN 979-8-9978331-0-7

The opinions in this manual are the author's own and do not represent an official position of the author's employer. The credit risk concerns discussed here are general observations about the indirect lending market, not a claim about any specific credit union's current portfolio or underwriting practices.

Case studies throughout this book are illustrative composites built to demonstrate a pattern, not documentation of a specific credit union, dealer, or event, unless a case study explicitly states that it is drawn from public court records or another named source. Any figures within a case study (dollar amounts, percentages, loan counts) are illustrative and should not be read as reported industry data.

Table of Contents

Acknowledgments

This book is the product of a long and rewarding career, and it would not exist without the support, guidance, and encouragement of many people along the way.

First and foremost, to my wife and family: thank you for your patience, support, encouragement, and love through the many phases of this work and this career. You mean the world to me.

To my closest friend and honorary brother, Bob Shaffer, thank you for always being there with steady counsel, honest perspective, and unwavering encouragement through every chapter of my career and my life.

To the many managers, peers, and team members I have had the honor of working alongside over 45 years, thank you for your wisdom, camaraderie, and shared commitment to excellence. Much of what I have learned about credit unions, leadership, risk, and service came from working with and learning from you.

Finally, to the credit union leaders and practitioners who read this book, thank you for the work you do every day to balance growth, service, and sound judgment. I hope these pages help make that work a little clearer and a little easier.

About This Book

This book lays out a single framework for how credit union leaders should evaluate, build, expand, or reassess an indirect auto lending program. Each chapter stands on its own as a reference, and together they build from the initial strategic decision through daily portfolio management.

Throughout this book, numeric thresholds, credit tiers, advance limits, and examples are used to show how disciplined indirect-lending decisions can be structured. They are not intended as model policy language or universal recommendations. Each credit union should adapt them to its charter, market, capital position, legal constraints, risk appetite, and portfolio history.

The chapters are organized to be read in order by a credit union building a program from the ground up, or used individually as a reference once a program is already running. The overview below shows how the eight chapters fit together. Chapters 1 and 2 are written for the board and the executive team making the go or no-go decision. Chapters 3 through 8 are written for the management team that has to build and run the program, with the board-level takeaways preserved in each chapter's summary, discussion questions, and action items.

Companion materials referenced throughout this book are available at https://mycurisk.com/volume. This QR code will take you there.

How This Book Is Organized

- Chapter 1: The Strategic Case for Indirect Auto Lending. Should your credit union be in indirect auto lending at all, and on what terms. Establishes the prime and super-prime, franchise-first framework recommended for a new program, and the boundary conditions every later chapter builds on. Companion resources: the Indirect Lending Readiness Checklist and the Indirect Lending Risk Assessment.
- Chapter 2: Market Feasibility and Strategy Definition. Whether a realistic opportunity exists in your specific market before you spend money on technology, staffing, or dealer visits, including dealer density, competitive landscape (Ally, GM Financial, Toyota Financial, banks, fintechs), the signals that indicate the answer may be not to build, and a starting framework for setting rate by credit tier from a risk-free benchmark. Companion resource: the CEO Self-Assessment.
- Chapter 3: Board Approval and Policy Development. Turning the strategic framework into board-approved underwriting standards and policy. Companion resources: the Indirect Lending Risk Assessment, the Board and Management Discussion Guide, and the Board Exercise.
- Chapter 4: Technology Infrastructure. Whether the current core and LOS can actually support an indirect program, the aggregator-to-LOS integration friction that follows, and the practical technology decisions a credit union has to make to originate and fund indirect paper.

- Chapter 5: Compliance and Legal Review. Reg Z, Reg B and ECOA dealer markup exposure, state RISA requirements, and the Military Lending Act purchase-money exemption and its limits.
- Chapter 6: Staffing and Dealer Relationship Management (DRM). Building the internal team, the consultant-for-guidelines boundary (a third party can implement your underwriting guidelines within a tight exception band, never hold full decisioning authority), and the risk of a DRM effectively coaching a dealer.
- Chapter 7: Dealer Onboarding and Launch. Dealer agreement terms, recourse and buyback triggers, and the mechanics of bringing a vetted dealer network live.
- Chapter 8: Dealer Performance Monitoring. Dealer incentive programs, EPD tracking, and why awards from a dealer or industry group are a warning sign to investigate, not a validation to celebrate. Companion resource: the Dealer Scorecard Tool.

Each chapter closes the same way: the failures that cause the most trouble in practice, a chapter summary, board discussion questions, and CEO action items. Terms used throughout the book are defined in the Glossary of Terms at the back, with a reference to the chapter that introduces each one.

Chapter 1: The Strategic Case for Indirect Auto Lending

Two Decisions, Not One

Strategic plans often have a line that looks familiar by the third year: grow auto loans. Sometimes it is a real strategy. Sometimes it is a wish carried forward from last year's plan, and the year before that, present on paper but never converted into a decision with limits, tradeoffs, and accountability. If that sounds familiar, you are not alone. In a late 2024 survey of credit union professionals, only 42 percent reported year-over-year growth in overall loan volume. The rest were flat or declining.

That gap usually comes down to whether the credit union ever made an actual decision, with boundaries attached, instead of carrying loan growth as a goal nobody defined the terms of. Credit unions often default to thinking about indirect lending as a choice between caution and ambition: stay out, and you are being conservative; get in, and you are chasing growth. That framing is wrong, and it is why so many indirect programs end up either underbuilt or overextended.

The real question is on what terms to compete for these loans, and whether your credit union can actually win the segment it decides to pursue. That is two decisions, not one. The first is where you draw the boundaries. The second is whether the program can work in your market. This chapter is where the first decision gets made deliberately.

The Go, No-Go Decision

With that first decision in view, this chapter asks the question that must be answered before any operational work begins: should your credit union be in the indirect auto lending business at all, and if so, on what terms? Everything else in this book, policy development, technology selection, dealer onboarding, staffing, ongoing monitoring, assumes that decision has been made deliberately. Some credit unions avoid the channel out of caution and lose the auto lending relationship anyway. Others expand into it during good years without the underwriting discipline to survive the downturn that eventually follows every credit cycle. This chapter is meant to keep either outcome from happening by forcing the boundary conversation first.

This book is written for the credit union caught between those two outcomes: not naive about the risk indirect lending carries, but not yet equipped with a clear framework for deciding how far into the channel to go. Each chapter in this series is written to stand on its own, so if you are picking this up out of order, or returning to it later as a reference rather than reading straight through, you should not need the rest of the book to use what is here.

This chapter is written for the people who have to make or approve the go, no-go decision: the CEO, the CFO, the VP of Lending, and the board members who will ultimately own the risk on the balance sheet. It will not give you the complete operational playbook. Policy language, dealer agreements, technology selection, and staffing decisions all come later, and they only make sense once the strategic boundaries in this chapter are set. What this chapter gives you is the decision framework and the two boundary conditions, credit tier and dealer type, that should shape every operational decision that follows it.

The stakes are real enough to justify spending real time here before moving on. NCUA has stated directly, in its own guidance, that it has seen seemingly healthy credit unions fail within months because an indirect lending program spun out of control. That outcome is entirely avoidable with the right boundaries set at the start.

The Reality of Today's Auto Finance Market

Indirect auto lending did not start as a lending strategy. It started as a dealer financing convenience, and it has grown into the dominant path by which most consumers finance a vehicle. Twenty years ago, a member deciding how to pay for a car had real reasons to visit their credit union first: better rates, a relationship, sometimes the only source of credit they trusted. That calculus has shifted. Today the member is standing in the dealer's finance office, the deal is already being run through an aggregator like CUDL, RouteOne, or Dealertrack, and multiple lenders are competing in real time to fund that specific vehicle before the member ever picks up the phone.

For most credit unions, the indirect channel is no longer a supplement to the direct auto lending business; increasingly, it is the auto lending business. A credit union that treats indirect as optional is choosing to compete for a shrinking share of a market that has already moved to the point of sale.

It also helps to be honest about who you are competing against on that aggregator platform: mostly captive finance arms such as GM Financial and Toyota Financial Services, along with large regional and national banks and an expanding set of fintech lenders. Captive lenders may have deeper dealer relationships, faster decisioning, and the ability to subsidize rates through the manufacturer to move inventory. Your realistic win rate on any given deal is a function of how competitive your rate and turnaround time are relative to that full field, not relative to other credit unions.

Every credit union that builds an indirect program is also making a tradeoff, and it is better discussed up front than discovered two years in. Indirect lending is transactional. The member relationship starts and often ends with the loan. You are not going to see the cross-sell rates, the multi-product relationships, or the loyalty that comes from a member who walked into a branch and sat down with a loan officer. What you get instead is loan growth, yield, and, done well, a funnel: some percentage of indirect borrowers will become full members over time, particularly if the onboarding and servicing experience is good.

In my experience, indirect volume also builds plain market awareness. It is common to hear "I have, or had, an auto loan with you" from someone who has never once walked into a branch. That kind of name recognition will not show up in any membership metric, but it is a real side effect. A board approving an indirect program should do so with this tradeoff clearly understood. Indirect lending grows the balance sheet. It does not, on its own, grow engaged membership. Confusing the two leads to disappointment that has nothing to do with credit performance and everything to do with mismatched expectations at the board table.

The Core Strategy for Disciplined Indirect Lending

Here is where a disciplined credit union should land, and why.

The question is not whether to chase indirect volume. It is whether the credit union can enter the channel with boundaries that protect the balance sheet: prime and super-prime credit, a franchise-first dealer posture, clear concentration limits, and the discipline to walk away from volume that does not fit.

> KEY PRINCIPLE
>
> **Opting out of indirect lending is not a more conservative auto lending strategy. It is largely an exit from auto lending, because that is where the transaction now happens.**

Prime and Super-Prime as the Starting Point

For a credit union building or resetting an indirect program, start in prime and super-prime credit, north of 680 FICO, and treat any move beyond it as a deliberate later decision, not a default to expand into once volume is flowing.

The growth in indirect lending over the last several years has come disproportionately from lenders willing to go deep into the credit spectrum, and the yields on that paper look attractive against a spreadsheet. They do not hold up through a downturn, for a specific structural reason.

Federally chartered credit unions are generally subject to a 15 percent federal interest-rate ceiling under the Federal Credit Union Act unless NCUA authorizes a higher temporary ceiling. NCUA has repeatedly authorized an 18 percent ceiling, and the current authorization has been extended through September 10, 2027. Confirm the current authorization window before relying on that date.

A finance company or bank without that ceiling can price a high-risk auto loan at 24, 27, even 29 percent to cover the losses that deep subprime paper generates when unemployment rises and vehicle values fall. A credit union capped at 18 percent cannot price for that same risk. That constraint is federal, not universal.

State-chartered credit unions operate under whatever rate authority their own state grants, and it varies widely from state to state. Virginia is a useful example: state-chartered credit unions there are exempt from the state's usury cap entirely and may charge whatever rate a borrower agrees to.

A state-chartered credit union in a state with that kind of latitude faces a different calculus than a federally chartered one boxed in at 18 percent, so check your own state's rules before assuming the federal ceiling applies to you.

When loss rates on that paper catch up to where they belong, as they eventually will, the credit union that wrote it may be left holding a rate that was never enough to cover it. Prime and super-prime credit does not have this problem, because the underlying risk is lower to begin with.

A credit union can responsibly go deeper, but that decision should be made deliberately, with pricing, capital, and monitoring built for that risk, by a program that has already proven it can execute cleanly at the prime tier, not backed into as volume grows.

Case Study: The Yield That Didn't Survive the Cycle

A federally chartered credit union with a healthy, conservatively underwritten indirect portfolio decides to widen its underwriting standards. Management is not reckless, the decision is made deliberately, in a strong economy, with loan growth targets the board has approved. The credit union begins approving paper two tiers deeper into the credit spectrum than its original policy allowed, priced at the 18 percent ceiling. On a spreadsheet, the math looks sound. The yield is well above the credit union's cost of funds, and early delinquency looks normal because early delinquency always looks normal in a strong economy.

Eighteen months later, unemployment ticks up and used vehicle values soften. The paper written at the loosest end of those widened standards starts defaulting at a rate the 18 percent ceiling was never priced to absorb. A finance company competing for the same borrowers could have charged 26 or 27 percent for that risk and still made money through the downturn. The credit union, capped by law at 18 percent, cannot. The losses land on a book that looked profitable for the better part of two years.

Nothing about the underwriting was fraudulent or careless in the moment. The problem was structural: the credit union priced deep subprime risk at a rate that was only ever sufficient for prime and super-prime credit, because federal law does not give it another option.

> **Lesson: A federally chartered credit union's 18 percent ceiling is not a pricing choice, it is a hard constraint. Deep subprime risk needs a rate the ceiling cannot supply, and the gap does not show up until the cycle turns.**

There is a second reason to stay out of deep subprime beyond the math. When losses in that segment show up industry-wide, examiners move to shut the activity down, sometimes at a single credit union, sometimes through broader supervisory pressure on the asset class as a whole. A program built up during good years and forced into retreat during bad ones never gains real traction. Dealers stop sending volume to a lender that disappears every downturn, and the credit union ends up rebuilding its dealer relationships from scratch each cycle instead of compounding the ones it already has.

When Direct Lending Better Serves the Member

The credit union mission includes serving members whose circumstances may require more than a fast, transaction-based credit decision. That mission does not disappear when the credit union enters indirect lending.

It does, however, require discipline about which channel is best suited to the member's situation and the credit union's ability to understand the full risk picture.

When a member's situation calls for more context, direct lending is usually the stronger and more mission-aligned channel. A direct loan gives the credit union a one-on-one conversation with the member, a clearer view of income, housing, household obligations, transportation needs, and available support, and a better opportunity to structure the loan around the member's actual ability to repay. It also creates a working relationship that can matter later if the member experiences hardship and needs help before delinquency becomes unmanageable.

The indirect channel is different. The application arrives through a dealer whose primary goal is completing the vehicle sale, not building a long-term financial relationship between the borrower and the credit union. The credit union receives a transaction, not the full member story. That makes it a poor default channel for stretching credit standards in the name of mission.

Members who need a closer review should not automatically be excluded from indirect lending, but the program should approach those transactions carefully and sparingly, with boundaries that make sense. A borrower within the credit union's immediate service area, or connected through a select employee group or other known affiliation, presents a different relationship opportunity than a distant borrower whose only connection to the credit union is a dealer-filed application. In those narrower circumstances, the credit union may have a practical way to know, reach, and support the member after funding.

The mission is to serve members responsibly, in a way that gives both the member and the credit union the best chance of success. For many members whose circumstances require relationship-based underwriting, that means preserving direct lending as the primary path and using indirect lending only when the relationship, geography, and underwriting support it.

Franchise Dealers as the Default, Independent Dealers as Exceptions

The default dealer strategy for a new indirect program should be franchise-first, with independent dealers treated as deliberate exceptions rather than a parallel starting network. Franchise dealerships are not inherently safe, and independent dealers are not inherently unsafe; the difference is structure. Franchise stores generally operate inside a more visible and accountable environment: manufacturer oversight, standardized vehicle-history expectations, certified pre-owned processes, brand reputation, and clearer escalation paths when something goes wrong. That structure does not eliminate fraud, documentation defects, or poor transaction quality, but it gives a new or disciplined program a cleaner and more manageable starting perimeter.

Independent dealers require a different standard because the credit union is relying more heavily on its own due diligence and ongoing monitoring. Some markets include long-established independent dealers with strong documentation, low complaint activity, stable ownership, and a reputation that justifies consideration. Even then, the relationship should begin as limited, closely monitored, and easy to unwind. The reason is not only collateral risk. When the credit union purchases a consumer credit contract, the seller's disclosures, vehicle representations, title practices, and after-sale conduct can follow the loan onto the credit union's books. Under the FTC's Holder Rule (16 CFR Part 433), the holder of the contract is subject to the same claims and defenses the buyer could raise against the seller. A direct loan does not carry that same exposure. You underwrite the borrower; you do not inherit the seller's conduct.

KEY PRINCIPLE

When you make a direct loan, you own the lending decision. When you buy a contract from a dealer, even an exceptional one, you own the entire transaction, including whatever the dealer failed to disclose.

Case Study: The Contract That Outlived the Dealer

A credit union approves indirect financing through a well-regarded independent dealer it has worked with for several years. The relationship has been clean: clear titles, accurate vehicle history, no prior complaints. On the strength of that track record, the credit union extends the relationship rather than treating each transaction as an exception to be re-evaluated.

A member finances a used vehicle through that dealer. Months later, the member discovers the vehicle had been in a flood and the damage was never disclosed on the title history the dealer provided at the point of sale. By the time the member raises a complaint, the dealer has closed its doors and is no longer reachable.

Under the FTC's Holder Rule, the member's claim against the dealer follows the contract, and the contract sits on the credit union's books. The credit union, not the dealer, is now the party the member has a legitimate claim against, for a misrepresentation the credit union had no part in making and no practical way to have discovered at the time of purchase.

Nothing about how the credit union underwrote the borrower was wrong. The exposure came entirely from the collateral side of the transaction, and from a dealer relationship that had earned trust but was never a franchise store with a manufacturer standing behind it.

> **Lesson: A strong track record with an independent dealer reduces collateral risk, it does not eliminate the liability the Holder Rule attaches to the contract. That liability outlives the dealer relationship, even a good one.**

Strategic Considerations

At the strategic level, a board needs to understand a few things before it ever gets to policy detail.

- Indirect volume is fixed-rate, multi-year paper, and it needs to be evaluated against your funding mix and your interest rate risk position the same way any other fixed-rate asset class would be. A credit union funded heavily with short-term, rate-sensitive shares takes on real asset-liability mismatch risk by growing a large book of five to seven year fixed-rate auto paper, regardless of how strong the credit quality is.

- Concentration is a strategic limit before it is an operational one. What percentage of the loan portfolio, and what percentage of assets, are you willing to have in indirect paper. That is a board-level risk appetite question, not something that should be backed into by watching volume grow and setting a limit after the fact. It is also a line that should not move very far until the credit union has watched its own policy and practices perform through a full cycle, origination through payoff, which in this asset class runs seven to eight years. A program with that kind of proven track record can responsibly carry a heavier concentration than the same policy language would justify in a program's first few years. That capacity is earned, not assumed, and it is not the right posture for a credit union new to the channel.
- Capital and liquidity capacity should be part of the initial go or no-go conversation, not something addressed after the program is already approved. A credit union that is well capitalized and has demonstrated funding stability is in a very different position than one operating close to its regulatory minimums, even if both have identical underwriting standards.
- Indirect lending also sits at the intersection of several compliance regimes that Chapter 5 covers in depth: Regulation Z for the actual credit terms and disclosures, Regulation B and ECOA for fair

lending exposure, particularly around discretionary dealer markup, and state retail installment sales acts that govern the underlying dealer contract itself. One area worth mentioning early because it is commonly misunderstood: most purchase-money auto loans are exempt from the Military Lending Act's protections, since the statute excludes credit extended for the express purpose of financing a vehicle purchase and secured by that vehicle. That exemption has been tested and upheld even where the loan bundles in related costs like GAP coverage, but the exemption is narrower than many lenders assume, and it is the kind of detail worth getting precisely right rather than approximately right.

- State law can layer on additional restrictions of its own. California's Military and Veteran Consumer Protection Act, for example, effectively bars financing GAP coverage into a secured auto loan for a covered servicemember: doing so voids the lender's security interest in the vehicle. A dealer or aggregator platform that is not current on state-specific rules like this one can put a credit union into a compliance position it did not know it had.

Build, Buy Participations, or Stay Out of the Asset Class?

There are three real strategic paths: build an in-house indirect program, participate through loan participations, or decide not to enter the asset class at all. The right one depends on a small number of concrete factors.

1. Build in-house makes sense when the credit union has, or is willing to hire, underwriting staff with genuine indirect auto experience, has the asset size and capital position to absorb the fixed costs of building the program properly, and has a credible path to a franchise dealer network in its market.
2. Buy participations makes sense when the credit union wants exposure to the asset class and its yield without taking on the operational risk of building underwriting, dealer relationships, and monitoring capability from scratch. This is the right answer for a credit union that recognizes it does not have the staff experience to underwrite this well and is not in a position to acquire it quickly. Established indirect lenders with long, evaluable loss histories exist across the credit union space. Buying participations from one of them, after pulling and reviewing that history, is a fundamentally safer starting point than an inexperienced underwriter learning the asset class on the credit union's own balance sheet.
3. Stay out of the asset class is also a legitimate answer for a credit union whose risk appetite, capital position, or strategic priorities genuinely point elsewhere. The mistake is not choosing this path, it is drifting into indirect lending without ever having the conversation, or choosing to build in-house because it seemed like the default option rather than because the credit union was actually positioned to do it well.

Loan participations are discussed in this chapter because boards evaluating indirect lending should first understand that other loan growth strategies exist. This book does not attempt to serve as a guide to participation lending. Rather, participations are presented as one of several strategic alternatives that should be considered when determining whether an indirect lending program is the right fit for a credit union's objectives, risk appetite, and operational capabilities.

The Indirect Lending Risk Pyramid

One practical way for a board to hold all of this together is to think of indirect lending risk as a pyramid. Credit losses sit at the apex, because they are what finally appears in a delinquency or charge-off report. Everything that produced them was decided lower down: the strategy the board approved, the concentration it was willing to carry, the dealers it allowed into the network, and the operating controls that determine whether anyone notices a problem in time. A pyramid is read from the bottom up, and so is an indirect lending program.

Figure 1-1. Credit losses appear at the apex; the decisions that produce them are made in the layers beneath.

The five layers, from the foundation upward:

- **Strategy Risk:** entering, expanding, or defending the program without a clear reason for being in the channel, a defined target borrower, or a board-approved answer to build, buy participations, or stay out.
- **Concentration Risk:** allowing indirect balances, dealer exposure, geography, or fixed-rate auto paper to grow beyond the credit union's capital, liquidity, funding mix, or monitoring capacity.
- **Dealer Risk:** purchasing contracts through dealers whose conduct, documentation quality, collateral representations, ancillary-product practices,

complaint patterns, or exception activity create risk the credit union may not see until after funding.

- **Operational Risk:** relying on people, systems, vendors, funding workflows, documentation processes, or manual workarounds that cannot consistently execute the program the board approved, or cannot show management what the program is actually producing.
- **Credit Risk:** approving borrowers, structures, terms, or exceptions whose expected losses are not supported by pricing, reserves, underwriting standards, or the credit union's legal rate ceiling.

The layers do not fail in isolation, and they fail from the bottom up. A weak strategy permits concentration nobody set a limit for. Unchecked concentration decides how much a single dealer relationship can eventually cost. Dealer selection determines the quality of the paper arriving. Operational gaps determine whether anyone sees the pattern while there is still time to act on it. Credit losses are simply the last layer, and the first one anybody notices. By the time the evidence appears in delinquency and charge-offs, the decisions that produced it were usually made months or years earlier.

This framework is not invented from scratch. The same NCUA guidance referenced at the start of this chapter identifies a set of indirect lending warning signs: excessive concentration without adequate controls, inadequate portfolio analysis, high levels of first-payment default, insufficient documentation, and poor dealer management. Every one of those maps onto a layer beneath the apex, and not one of them is a credit underwriting failure. That is the useful part. The regulator's own warning list is built almost entirely out of the layers a credit union can still do something about.

Using the Pyramid as an Early Warning Tool

- The history of indirect auto lending is why the pyramid starts with strategy and concentration rather than with delinquency. Indirect auto portfolios, especially where credit tiers or dealer networks expanded during strong markets, produced materially higher losses during the 2008 to 2010 downturn and again during pandemic-era volatility in used vehicle values. The damage came less from indirect lending itself than from boundaries that had already eroded before the cycle turned.
- The first weakness usually appears near the base. A program may still look healthy by every normal performance measure while strategy risk, concentration risk, and dealer risk are already building underneath it. That is why a credit union can appear sound until the underlying program problems become visible all at once.
- The timing gap is what makes the pyramid a management tool rather than a diagram. The credit unions NCUA describes typically made the boundary-eroding decisions eighteen to thirty-six months before the losses showed up on a call report. By the time the numbers look bad, the risk has usually been accumulating for years.
- Incentive structure is the fastest single test of whether the pyramid is holding or starting to lean.

> A program that pays staff or dealers for indirect loan volume rather than loan performance is rewarding the apex while ignoring every layer that produces it.

None of this requires a credit union to be reckless or poorly managed. The pyramid usually begins to fail through ordinary discipline erosion in a good economy: small, individually defensible decisions that only add up to a problem once the cycle turns and the boundaries that should have held it are already gone.

Readiness Before Approval

Before a board approves an indirect program, or expands one that already exists, it should be able to answer a short set of questions without hedging.

Why are we doing this? Do we have staff with real indirect auto underwriting experience, not adjacent experience in mortgage or consumer direct lending? Do we understand, in specific numbers, what our concentration limits are and why we chose them? Do we have access to a credible franchise dealer network in our market, or are we assuming one exists without having tested it? Do we have a plan for post-funding monitoring that goes beyond watching delinquency roll in, including static pool analysis and early payment default tracking? And are we prepared to say no to dealer volume, or to a specific dealer relationship, if it stops meeting our standards, even when the numbers look good in the short term?

A credit union that cannot answer these questions with confidence is not ready to build, and should look seriously at the participation path instead.

The Indirect Lending Readiness Checklist puts these six questions in fillable form, with the pyramid layer each one tests, available with the other companion materials at https://mycurisk.com/volume.

The Indirect Lending Risk Assessment works through the same questions in structured form, layer by layer, and is available with the other companion materials at https://mycurisk.com/volume.

Things That Get Credit Unions Into Trouble

The strategic mistakes are rarely dramatic. They are decisions that each looked defensible at the time:

- Treating a decision to stay out of indirect lending as the conservative choice, and losing the auto lending relationship anyway.
- Approving the program as a membership growth strategy when it is a balance sheet growth strategy, and setting board expectations it was never going to meet.
- Moving deeper into the credit spectrum because the yield looks attractive, without first confirming the rate ceiling can price that risk through a downturn.
- Adding independent dealer relationships as a standing part of the network rather than as exceptions the credit union has evaluated and chosen.

- Using the indirect channel to serve members whose circumstances call for relationship-based underwriting, because it feels like the mission-aligned answer.
- Setting concentration limits after volume has arrived rather than before, and moving them because growth made the original number inconvenient.
- Choosing to build in-house because it seemed like the default option, without ever comparing it against buying participations.
- Delegating the go or no-go decision to a vendor, a platform, or a consultant with an interest in the answer.

None of these decisions requires a credit union to be reckless or poorly managed. Each one is a boundary set in this chapter being relaxed once, for a reason that made sense in the moment.

Chapter Summary

- Indirect lending is effectively the auto lending market now. Avoiding it isn't a more conservative strategy, it's largely an exit from the product.
- Indirect lending is transactional, not relationship-building. Treat it as balance sheet growth, not membership growth, and set board expectations accordingly.
- For a new program, stay in prime and super-prime credit, north of 680 FICO. The 18 percent federal rate ceiling can't price for deep subprime

risk through a downturn, and going deeper should be a deliberate later decision, not a default.

- Default to franchise dealerships, especially early on. Collateral fraud risk is lower and far easier to control than credit risk underwritten loan by loan, and a well-vetted independent relationship is an earned exception, not a starting point.
- Use direct lending, not the indirect channel, for members whose circumstances require relationship-based underwriting, except narrowly within your own service area or SEG affiliates.
- A direct loan puts you in the underwriting seat. An indirect contract purchase makes you liable for the dealer's conduct under the FTC Holder Rule, and that liability outlives the dealer relationship.
- The Indirect Lending Risk Pyramid gives the board a practical way to monitor discipline before losses appear. Read from the foundation up, the layers are strategy risk, concentration risk, dealer risk, operational risk, and credit risk, with credit losses at the apex because they surface last.
- NCUA's own indirect lending warning signs map almost entirely onto the layers beneath the apex. Not one of them is a credit underwriting failure, which is why board reporting should reach below delinquency.
- Concentration, capital, funding mix, credit-tier boundaries, dealer-type boundaries, and operating capacity need board-approved limits set before volume grows, not after.

- If you don't have the underwriting experience to do this well, buying participations from an established indirect lender is safer than building blind.
- Use the readiness assessment before approving or expanding a program, not after problems surface.

Board Discussion Questions

1. What is our stated position on serving members whose circumstances require relationship-based underwriting, and does our actual channel strategy match it?
2. Have we formally evaluated the participation alternative, or did we default to building in-house without comparing the two paths?
3. Is any part of our staff compensation tied to indirect loan volume, and if so, how are we controlling for the incentive that creates?
4. Which layer of the Indirect Lending Risk Pyramid would show stress first in our program, and what evidence would management bring to the board before delinquency or charge-offs made the problem obvious?
5. Can management show us where each of NCUA's indirect lending warning signs would appear in our own reporting, and which of them we are not currently able to see?
6. If our charter type or state usury limits cap how high we can price for risk, have we confirmed exactly where that ceiling falls, and have we

agreed which credit tiers we simply will not serve as a result?

7. Have we deliberately chosen franchise dealers as our starting network, or did that happen by default because a platform or vendor onboarded us that way?
8. Are we expecting this program to grow engaged membership, grow the balance sheet, or both, and have we been honest with each other at this table about which one it will actually do?
9. What specific evidence, and how much of it, would cause this board to decide the program should shrink or shut down rather than continue at its current scale?
10. Do we understand what the Holder Rule means for our own liability exposure on a contract we purchase, in concrete terms, not as a compliance footnote?

CEO Action Items

1. Confirm the credit union's current FICO floor and dealer network policy in writing, check both against the recommendations in this chapter, and document any deviation as a deliberate board or management decision rather than something the program drifted into.
2. Complete the Indirect Lending Risk Assessment before approving or expanding the program, using it to test each layer of the pyramid in the order it is built: strategy, concentration, dealer, operational, and credit risk. A companion

template is provided at https://mycurisk.com/volume.

3. Prepare a one-page strategic recommendation for the board that states whether management recommends building in-house, buying participations, or staying out of the asset class, and identifies the evidence supporting that recommendation.
4. Ask ALCO or the appropriate balance sheet committee to model the effect of the proposed indirect portfolio on funding mix, liquidity, fixed-rate concentration, and interest rate risk before any program expansion is approved.
5. Direct management to document the program's initial concentration limits, credit-tier boundaries, and dealer-type boundaries as decision criteria, not merely operating preferences, so future growth can be measured against the original strategy.
6. Require a pre-launch evidence package showing that the credit union has the underwriting experience, capital capacity, liquidity capacity, and dealer-network access needed to execute the chosen path without relying on optimistic volume assumptions.

Chapter 2: Market Feasibility and Strategy Definition

Test the Market Before You Build

Most credit unions that get into indirect lending skip one essential step: they start building before confirming whether their market can support the program they want.

Market feasibility is the first risk control because it tests the opportunity before the credit union commits money, staff time, technology, and dealer relationships to a program that may not fit its market.

> KEY PRINCIPLE
>
> **The goal of a feasibility study is not to prove indirect lending can work. The goal is to determine whether it can work in your market, with your staff, and within your underwriting standards and risk appetite.**

Feasibility Is a Risk Management Exercise

Many institutions treat feasibility studies as justification documents. Management already wants the program, so the research becomes a way to support a decision that has effectively already been made.

A useful feasibility process does the opposite. It begins with the assumption that the answer may be no.

That mindset matters. If the only acceptable outcome is "yes," negative information will be minimized. Dealer satisfaction will be interpreted as interest. Market volume will be mistaken for available opportunity. Competitive pressure will be underestimated. Operational capacity will be assumed rather than measured.

A genuine feasibility review asks whether the opportunity is real, whether the credit union can compete for the right loans, and whether the resulting program would be consistent with the institution's underwriting standards, risk appetite, and capacity.

A negative feasibility result may be the most valuable outcome of the process, because it prevents the institution from investing scarce resources into a program that was never likely to produce acceptable results.

Start With the Market You Can Actually Serve

A disciplined credit union does not need to compete everywhere. In fact, it usually should not.

Indirect lending platforms can make a credit union visible to dealers across a wide geography. That visibility may sound attractive, especially when management is focused on loan growth. But a broader approved dealer network creates broader problems: more applications, more unfamiliar dealers, more distant borrowers, more funding activity, and less practical ability to build meaningful relationships.

The first feasibility question should not be, "How many dealers can we reach?"

The better question is, "Which dealers and borrowers are actually within our natural market?"

For many credit unions, the natural market generally includes local franchise dealers, adjacent communities, existing service areas, and markets where the institution has some realistic ability to maintain borrower relationships after funding.

KEY PRINCIPLE

Just because a platform can open your program to every approved dealer does not mean your credit union should allow it.

Geographic Discipline

Geographic discipline is a form of capacity discipline. Opening an indirect program to every available dealer can expose the credit union to volume it cannot process and borrowers it cannot reasonably serve.

Loans booked far outside the credit union's natural footprint may also be more vulnerable to early payoff. A borrower may already have a relationship with a bank or credit union closer to home. After the vehicle purchase is complete, that borrower may refinance the loan with the institution they already use or the institution physically closer to their daily life.

The credit union may have already underwritten the file, processed the contract, funded the loan, booked the system record, and paid the dealer incentive. If the loan pays off shortly afterward, the booked balance may never generate enough value to justify the work required to produce it.

Borrowers outside the immediate market need not be rejected outright, but geographic reach should be intentional, not accidental.

Identify Your Competitive Advantage

A credit union operating in higher-credit-quality lending is usually not going to win every deal on rate. Captive finance companies and large lenders may use subsidized pricing, promotional programs, and broad marketing budgets that many credit unions cannot match.

That reality should not discourage management. It should sharpen the strategy.

For many credit unions, the better opportunity may be used vehicles sold through franchise dealerships. New vehicle transactions are often influenced by manufacturer incentives and captive finance programs. Used vehicle transactions may present a different competitive environment, especially when the credit union can provide reliable decisions, consistent funding, and underwriting standards that fit strong borrowers.

A disciplined lender does not need to become the dealer's answer for every transaction. It needs to identify the segment where it can compete profitably and consistently: loans that fit its credit standards, can be processed within its capacity, and produce value after funding and early-payoff risk are considered.

Possible advantages may include responsiveness, consistency, access to experienced decision makers, local reputation, simple funding expectations, or stable underwriting standards that do not change every month.

Credit unions should not underestimate the value of predictability. Dealers may tolerate a decline, a stipulation, or a counteroffer. What they dislike is uncertainty.

A lender that approves quickly but funds slowly will eventually damage its reputation. A lender that opens aggressively and then retreats when volume becomes unmanageable will be viewed as inconsistent. A lender that changes underwriting standards without warning will lose trust.

For a lender without captive-finance scale, reputation is often built less on size and more on being consistent and predictable. Dealers may not remember your lowest rate from six months ago. They will remember whether you funded on time, whether you returned calls, whether your standards changed unexpectedly, and whether your approval process was consistent.

KEY PRINCIPLE

A lender's reputation is not built on volume alone. It is built on predictability.

Pull Real Market Data Before Building Anything

Assumptions are not a feasibility study.

Management should review available market intelligence before investing heavily in technology, staffing, vendor contracts, or dealer outreach. In practice, that may mean using detailed registration, transaction, valuation, and competitive-market data from sources such as Autocount, J.D. Power, and S&P Global Mobility, along with dealer platform reporting and the credit union's own member data. The purpose is to ground the decision in evidence before committing resources, while the decision itself stays with the credit union. The specific provider matters less than whether the data is current, granular, and matched to the market segment the credit union actually intends to serve.

The key is to look beyond total volume. Total market volume can be misleading. A region may generate substantial auto loan activity while still offering very little opportunity for the credit union's intended underwriting standards.

The better analysis asks:

- Which dealers produce the type of loans we want?
- Which lenders currently dominate those dealers?
- Are those lenders winning because of rate, speed, advance rate, incentives, stipulation flexibility, or existing relationships?
- What share of the business appears to involve higher-credit-quality borrowers?
- How much of the opportunity is new vehicle business influenced by manufacturer incentives?
- How much is used vehicle business where a credit union may have a more realistic opportunity?

Where loans go tells management what dealers value. The feasibility process should identify not only who is winning, but why.

Case Study: The Market That Looked Better on Paper

A credit union reviews regional auto loan data and sees substantial vehicle financing activity. The opportunity appears attractive. Several franchise dealers in the area produce meaningful monthly volume, and management believes capturing even a small share would materially improve loan growth.

The detail underneath is less encouraging. Most new vehicle financing is dominated by captive lenders using promotional rates. A large share of used vehicle financing is already controlled by two aggressive lenders willing to approve higher advance rates and broader credit tiers than the credit union is willing to accept. The dealers with the highest volume are not necessarily producing the loans the credit union wants.

The market is active, but the credit union's realistic opportunity is narrower than management first assumed.

> **Lesson: Market volume is not the same as market opportunity.**

Talk to Dealers Before You Talk to Vendors

Data tells you where loans are flowing. Dealers tell you why.

After reviewing market data, management should identify three to five dealerships it would realistically want in the approved dealer network and speak with the F&I managers. These conversations should be listening exercises, not sales calls.

The goal of these conversations is to understand what frustrates them about the lenders they already use and whether those frustrations create a legitimate opening.

A short, consistent questionnaire usually works better than a casual conversation because it allows management to compare responses across dealers.

Questions might include:

- What operational issue causes the most frustration with your current lenders?
- Which stipulations create the most friction?
- When lenders offer similar rates, what determines who receives the contract?
- How important are evening or weekend decisioning support?
- How easy is it to reach someone who can resolve a stalled transaction?
- What causes you to stop sending applications to a lender?
- If you could change one thing about your current lending partners, what would it be?

Patterns matter more than individual answers. One dealer complaint may only reflect preference. The same complaint from multiple dealers may identify a real market gap.

Case Study: Courtesy Is Not Commitment

A credit union schedules meetings with several local dealers. The conversations are friendly. F&I managers say they would "love to have another credit union option" and encourage the institution to join the platform.

Management initially interprets the feedback as market demand. A more disciplined review asks follow-up questions: How many applications would they realistically send? Which types of borrowers? Under what circumstances would they choose the credit union over their current lenders? What existing frustrations would the credit union solve?

The answers are vague. Dealers are willing to add the credit union as another option, but no one identifies a specific reason the credit union would regularly win the loans.

> **Lesson: Dealer courtesy is not the same as dealer commitment.**

Start Rate Setting From the Risk-Free Benchmark

Competing on predictability rather than rate does not mean rate does not matter. Knowing whether the credit union can actually compete, the feasibility question this chapter opened with, depends on knowing what a defensible rate looks like before comparing it to a competitor's. Market competition alone is not a sufficient basis for setting one. The starting point should be financial conditions, not what a competitor happens to be advertising this month.

A practical benchmark is the two-year Treasury yield, used here as an opportunity-cost floor rather than a replacement for cost of funds. Cost of funds and the Treasury benchmark answer different questions, and they should stay separate: cost of funds is what the money actually costs the credit union today, while the Treasury yield is the return available on a similar-duration alternative if that money were not lent out at all. A rate that fails to clear the Treasury benchmark is turning down a safer return to take on credit risk, regardless of what cost of funds happens to be at the time. Most indirect auto paper carries a weighted average life of roughly two to three years, which makes the two-year Treasury a reasonable proxy for that comparison. Rate setting starts there, not at zero.

From that benchmark, each credit tier needs its own margin built up from real costs, not a flat markup applied across the board:

- Dealer participation or reserve, the compensation paid for the paper.
- Expected loan losses for that specific credit tier, not a portfolio-wide average.
- Administrative and servicing costs, including the cost of collections on the accounts that go delinquent.
- A profit margin the credit union is comfortable defending to its own board.

Built this way, the resulting rate is a number the credit union can defend, tier by tier, with its own assumptions in view, rather than a guess or whatever the competitive market happens to be charging. That also makes the same framework useful in the other direction: when a competitor's advertised rate looks unbeatable, running it back through this structure is usually the fastest way to see whether that rate reflects a real cost advantage or an underpriced risk the competitor has not fully accounted for yet.

Figure 2-1. The same components build every tier's rate; the expected loss for the tier is what actually moves. Amounts are illustrative, not recommended pricing.

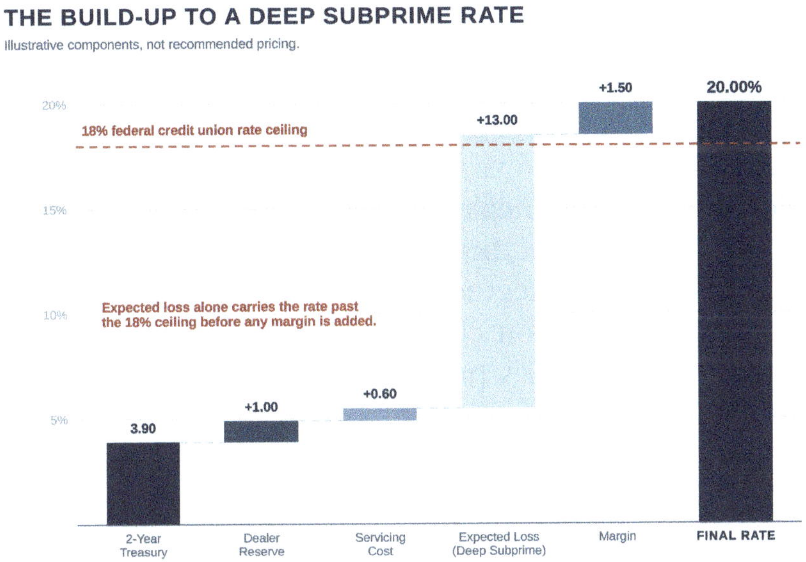

This is also the arithmetic behind Chapter 1's claim that the 18 percent federal rate ceiling cannot price deep subprime risk. Run a deep subprime tier through the same four components (dealer participation, a materially higher expected loss rate, the same servicing and collection costs, and a minimum acceptable margin), and the rate that tier actually requires clears 18 percent before profit is even added back in. At that point the ceiling stops being a policy preference: the build-up returns a number the credit union is not permitted to charge.

Dealer participation or reserve, the first component above, is more than a cost to plug in. Chapter 5's discussion of dealer markup and pricing discretion governs how that compensation may be structured (flat, capped, or tightly tiered), and why unmeasured discretion there creates fair lending exposure. A rate sheet built from this framework still has to satisfy that constraint.

The same four components that build a rate also build a return. Once a tier's expected loss, servicing and collection cost, and dealer participation are known, what remains after subtracting them from the rate charged is the loan's actual expected margin, before overhead. A rate that clears the Treasury benchmark on paper can still be a weak loan once early payoff attrition is factored in: a loan that pays off in eighteen months earns eighteen months of margin, not the full term the rate was built to recover over.

Capacity Discipline Belongs in the Feasibility Study

Loan volume can be a friend or a foe for any lender without matching operating capacity.

A successful launch can create problems if approvals exceed the credit union's ability to underwrite, process, fund, and service the loans. This is especially true in indirect lending because dealer expectations are immediate.

The tolerance line described earlier in this chapter applies directly here. A dealer will absorb a decline or a stipulation, but slow funding and unexplained delays are exactly the kind of uncertainty that costs a lender its reputation.

Large lenders may have more tools to recover from inconsistency. They can often add resources, run promotions, or shift volume across a broader footprint. A lender with limited operating capacity usually has fewer options. Its best competitive asset is consistency.

That means feasibility should include capacity analysis before launch.

- How many applications can staff review in a normal day?
- How many funded contracts can be processed without delay?
- What happens if volume doubles unexpectedly?
- Who clears stipulations when key staff are out?
- How long can the credit union maintain dealer responsiveness during vacations, holidays, or system interruptions?
- Does liquidity planning support the projected booking volume?

Wanting the loans is easy. The harder question is whether the credit union can responsibly handle them.

Case Study: Predictability During a Staffing Crisis

During the COVID-19 pandemic, many lenders experienced the same problem at the same time: strong loan demand combined with extended staffing shortages.

At one credit union, management recognized that funding timelines would likely exceed normal expectations. The institution could continue approving loans and allow dealers to discover the funding delay after assigning the contract, or it could disclose the expected delay before the dealer made that decision.

Management chose the second option.

A stipulation was added to all approvals advising dealers that funding could be delayed by approximately seven to fourteen days due to limited staffing.

That delay did not meet the credit union's own service standard. It was not the level of performance the institution wanted to provide. But it did support something equally important: predictability.

Dealers knew the expected funding timeline before assigning the loan. That allowed them to proceed with the credit union, choose another lender, or make other arrangements with full knowledge of the likely delay.

Most dealer frustration comes from uncertainty rather than bad news. A delayed funding timeline can often be managed if it is disclosed early. An unexpected delay after assignment damages trust.

> **Lesson: During periods of operational stress, predictability becomes more valuable than speed.**

Define the Initial Approved Dealer Network

One of the most important launch decisions is deciding where the program will not be available.

Indirect platforms may allow a lender to appear broadly to approved dealers. That should not be the default for a disciplined program. A narrow, intentional approved dealer network provides better volume control, better relationship management, and better alignment with the credit union's service area.

The initial approved dealer network should generally prioritize local or nearby franchise dealers, dealers with strong reputations, dealers whose customer base overlaps the credit union's field of membership or service area, and dealers that management can realistically visit and monitor.

Expansion should be earned, not assumed.

> KEY PRINCIPLE
>
> **Start narrow. Prove the process. Expand deliberately.**

Case Study: The Approved Dealer Network That Was Too Broad

A credit union joins an indirect platform and initially makes itself available to a broad approved dealer network. Application volume arrives quickly, but much of it comes from dealers outside the credit union's natural service area.

The credit union spends time reviewing unfamiliar dealers, unfamiliar buyer patterns, and distant borrowers unlikely to develop broader relationships. Some loans pay off early when borrowers refinance with institutions closer to home. Staff capacity is consumed, but strategic value is limited.

The problem was not that the platform generated activity. The problem was that the credit union allowed activity to substitute for strategy.

> **Lesson: Access to a broad dealer network is not the same as a strategy for using it.**

Marginal Volume and "Let's See What Sticks" Lenders

There is another reality many new indirect lenders eventually discover. When a lender first enters the market, some dealerships use it as a "let's see what sticks" lender. Applications may begin arriving that have already been declined by several other lenders. Transactions outside normal underwriting standards may appear in meaningful volume.

A new lender should expect some of this activity. It should not accept the idea that buying a few marginal loans is the unavoidable price of entering the market.

Approving two or three marginal loans does not automatically cause a dealer to begin sending stronger loans later. Buying marginal risk is not a marketing strategy. It is simply buying marginal risk.

That does not mean a lender should never help a dealer solve a difficult transaction. There may be times when assistance makes sense. The difference is timing and relationship quality. A lender might reasonably extend assistance to a dealership looking for a reasonable home for a marginal transaction, but that assistance should come after an established relationship with good quality, consistent volume, and mutual trust, not before.

Indirect lending is a two-way street. Partnerships are built on mutual benefit. If a dealership consistently sends loans that fit your underwriting standards, support your portfolio objectives, and create value for both organizations, helping them occasionally solve an unusual situation may be appropriate. If the relationship consists entirely of exceptions, there is no partnership. There is only risk.

KEY PRINCIPLE

Do not assume poor-quality volume is an unavoidable cost of entering the indirect market.

Accept the Answer

This may be the most important part of the feasibility process.

If the data shows the market is saturated, if dealers are satisfied with existing lenders, if the available opportunity requires credit risk outside the board's appetite, or if internal capacity cannot support the program, then the correct answer may be no.

That answer can be difficult to accept, especially once management has invested time in discussing the program. But declining to build a weak program is not a lack of ambition. It is risk discipline.

Sometimes the best feasibility outcome is a decision to pursue loan participations instead of building a direct dealer program. Sometimes the correct decision is to strengthen direct auto lending first. Sometimes management should revisit the opportunity later after staffing, liquidity, technology, or market conditions change.

The feasibility process exists to support an informed decision, not to create momentum.

A Test Before the Recommendation

Before management recommends an indirect program to the board, the CEO should be able to make a short set of statements plainly, without qualification. We know which market segment we are trying to win. We have objective data supporting the opportunity. We have spoken with dealers before committing to vendors or technology. We know why dealers would choose us. We have defined our initial approved dealer network. We understand our operational capacity, and we know how we will communicate its limits before they become service failures.

Three more statements matter most, because they are the ones a program under pressure abandons first. We know how we will respond to marginal application volume. We know what would cause us to say no. And we are prepared to accept a negative feasibility result.

A CEO who cannot make those last three statements has not completed a feasibility study. They have built a case.

The CEO Self-Assessment, a companion document to this chapter, puts these statements in fillable form with space to record the evidence behind each one, available at https://mycurisk.com/volume.

Things That Get Credit Unions Into Trouble

The most common feasibility mistakes are surprisingly simple:

- Building a program based on assumptions instead of evidence.

- Confusing dealer friendliness with dealer commitment.
- Looking only at total market volume instead of the specific segment the credit union intends to target.
- Opening the approved dealer network too broadly at launch.
- Ignoring geographic relationship risk.
- Underestimating funding, processing, and staffing capacity.
- Assuming rate alone will create sustainable dealer relationships.
- Mistaking marginal application volume for relationship development.
- Treating a feasibility study as a justification exercise rather than an evaluation exercise.

Programs built on guesses almost always disappoint. Programs built on evidence have a better chance of remaining disciplined when volume begins to arrive.

Chapter Summary

- Market feasibility is the discipline of deciding whether opportunity is real before the credit union commits resources. It requires more than enthusiasm, more than market volume, and more than friendly dealer conversations.
- The purpose is to determine whether an indirect program can work in the credit union's actual

market, with its actual staff, and within its actual underwriting standards and risk appetite.

- A disciplined credit union does not need to be everywhere, win every application, or match every competitor. It needs a narrow, realistic, manageable opportunity that produces value without overwhelming capacity or weakening discipline.
- A disciplined feasibility process also protects the institution from becoming a lender of last resort. New lenders should expect some marginal applications, but they should not mistake weak volume for relationship building. Strong dealer partnerships are built on mutual value, not mutual exceptions.
- The most disciplined decision may be to proceed. It may also be to wait, buy participations, narrow the scope, or decline to build the program at all. Any of those outcomes can be successful if the decision is based on evidence rather than momentum.
- Rate setting should start from a risk-free benchmark like the two-year Treasury yield, then build each credit tier's margin from dealer participation, tier-specific expected loss, servicing and collection cost, and profit, not from what a competitor happens to be advertising.

Board Discussion Questions

MARKET OPPORTUNITY

1. Do we have objective market data showing a realistic opportunity?
2. What specific segment of the market are we targeting?
3. Which lenders are currently winning those loans, and why?

COMPETITIVE POSITION

4. Are we relying on rate, responsiveness, consistency, local relationships, or another factor?
5. Would dealers have a clear reason to choose us over their current lenders?
6. Can management explain how each credit tier's rate was built, component by component, rather than pointing only to where it sits against competitors?

GEOGRAPHY AND DEALER SCOPE

7. What geographic area are we willing to serve through indirect lending?
8. How will we know when expansion is appropriate?

CAPACITY AND RISK APPETITE

9. How much application volume can we support without damaging service quality?

10. How much funding volume can we support without creating backlogs?
11. If the feasibility review produced a negative answer, would we be willing to accept it?

CEO Action Items

The CEO's role is to ensure that enthusiasm does not outrun evidence. Before recommending an indirect program to the board, complete the following actions.

1. **Define the intended market:** Identify the geographic footprint, dealer types, borrower profile, and vehicle segment the credit union intends to pursue.
2. **Gather objective market data:** Review available market reports, dealer platform data, internal member information, and any relevant competitive intelligence.
3. **Identify three to five target dealers:** Focus on dealers the credit union would actually want in the program, not every dealer the platform can reach.
4. **Conduct structured dealer interviews:** Use a consistent questionnaire and compare responses for patterns.
5. **Identify the competitive advantage:** Document why a dealer would choose the credit union when other lenders are available.
6. **Perform a capacity review:** Evaluate underwriting, processing, funding, dealer support, liquidity, and servicing capacity before launch.

7. **Define initial dealer-access limits:** Decide which dealers should be active at launch and which should remain outside the program unless expansion is later approved.
8. **Define the response to marginal volume:** Establish in advance how management will respond when dealers submit loans that have already been declined elsewhere or require repeated exceptions.
9. **Prepare a go/no-go recommendation:** Present the board with an honest recommendation that includes negative findings, unresolved concerns, and conditions for proceeding.
10. **Build a rate sheet by credit tier:** document each tier's Treasury benchmark, dealer participation, expected loss rate, servicing and collection cost, and margin, so the resulting rate can be defended component by component.

Chapter 3: Board Approval and Policy Development

Programs Become What Policy Allows

Every indirect lending program eventually becomes what its policy and operating framework allow in practice. Not what the board intended. Not what management envisioned. What the adopted boundaries, exceptions, reporting, and procedures permit once real dealer pressure begins.

Some programs start conservatively and remain disciplined through multiple credit cycles. Others begin with sensible underwriting standards and gradually move into risks nobody intended to take. Sometimes technology contributes. Sometimes dealer pressure contributes. Sometimes the cause is simply chasing volume at any price.

The common issue is governance. An indirect lending program begins long before the first application arrives from a dealership. It begins when the board decides what risks the credit union is willing to accept, which risks it is not, and how management will report when actual practices begin moving away from those decisions.

This is where the book shifts from board-level strategy to the management work that carries it out. The chapter does not attempt a complete underwriting manual, and the specific thresholds and examples in it are illustrative rather than prescriptive. Its purpose is to establish the governance framework that allows underwriting, technology, dealer relationships, and monitoring to operate inside clearly defined boundaries, and to show enough of the mechanics for a CEO to tell whether that framework is actually being executed. A good policy creates discipline. A poor policy creates surprises.

Policy Sets the Boundary. Management Builds the Road.

One of the most common governance mistakes is putting operating procedures into board policy. The board should not be deciding which income-estimation provider to use, which underwriting variables to review, which credit score model to obtain, or which stipulations belong on a particular loan. Those are management responsibilities.

The board should establish the credit union's risk appetite, broad credit-tier boundaries, concentration limits, exception authority, reporting expectations, review triggers, and transaction structures outside the institution's comfort level. Management should translate those boundaries into underwriting standards, automated decision rules, procedures, pricing tables, and approval authorities.

> KEY PRINCIPLE
>
> **Policy establishes the guardrails. Management builds and maintains the operating rules inside them.**

The goal is neither unlimited discretion nor a rigid rulebook that requires board approval for every operational change. The policy should be stable enough to guide the program through changing conditions while the supporting decision-rules document remains flexible enough for management to adjust implementation without changing the board's risk appetite.

A suggested split of board versus management responsibility is available with the companion materials at https://mycurisk.com/volume.

Developing Decision Rules: You Do Not Have to Invent Them Yourself

Many credit unions approach automated underwriting by starting with a handful of obvious criteria: credit score, loan-to-value ratio, prior bankruptcy history, or debt-to-income limits. While those factors matter, they are often only part of what actually predicts loan performance.

For a newly launched indirect program, management should consider whether outside expertise could improve the development of automated decision rules. Credit bureaus, lending consultants, and specialized analytics firms often maintain large datasets spanning multiple lenders, economic cycles, and geographic regions. Those datasets can identify credit attributes that are statistically correlated with future loan performance in ways that may not be obvious from a credit union's own limited portfolio history.

For example, a consultant may analyze national auto-loan performance data and identify combinations of bureau attributes, trade-line characteristics, utilization patterns, payment behavior, or credit-history indicators that consistently predict lower losses within a targeted credit tier. Depending on the engagement, the consultant may provide only the analytical findings and recommended metrics, or may go further by proposing a complete decision-rule framework aligned with the credit union's stated risk appetite.

The same point applies to the growing use of AI-driven or machine-learning credit decisioning systems. A number of specialized technology providers now offer platforms designed to analyze large data sets, identify predictive credit patterns, and support more refined automated decisioning than a traditional rule tree may allow. These systems can be serious and sophisticated tools, and many are well regarded in the industry. For a credit union without deep model-governance resources, however, the question is whether the institution has the budget, data quality, staff capacity, model-governance discipline, compliance oversight, and implementation support to use it responsibly.

This book does not attempt to evaluate those systems in detail or recommend one over another. The practical point is simpler: management should know that these tools exist, ask whether the current or prospective LOS can integrate with them, and preserve enough flexibility in the technology roadmap to add more advanced decisioning capability later if the program's size, risk profile, and resources eventually justify it. An AI decisioning platform is another tool, not a shortcut around underwriting discipline, and it must operate inside the board-approved risk appetite, the credit union's fair lending controls, and the practical limits of the systems and people expected to manage it.

This type of analysis can be especially valuable for a credit union entering indirect lending for the first time. A credit union may have excellent experience managing direct consumer loans while still lacking sufficient indirect-loan history to develop statistically reliable automated underwriting criteria on its own.

Management should also recognize an important limitation: the most predictive variable is not always a variable the loan origination system can use. A consultant may identify an attribute that has strong predictive value but cannot be imported, calculated, or evaluated within the decision engine. For that reason, technology capabilities should be discussed before the underwriting model is finalized.

Whenever possible, include representatives from the loan origination system, decision-engine provider, or implementation team in the consultation process. A rule that cannot be programmed cannot be automated. Early involvement helps ensure the final underwriting framework reflects both sound credit analytics and the practical realities of the institution's technology environment.

The objective is not to outsource the credit union's risk appetite. That remains management's responsibility and the board's oversight responsibility. The objective is to use available expertise to convert that risk appetite into decision rules that can be executed consistently, measured objectively, and refined over time based on actual portfolio performance.

The Exception Trap

Every indirect lender encounters applications that almost fit. The borrower may have strong income, a long employment history, or substantial equity, but one element falls outside the normal underwriting standards. That is where exceptions begin.

Exceptions are not inherently weak lending. Experienced judgment is one of the advantages a credit union can bring to indirect lending. The problem begins when exceptions become routine, concentrate at particular dealers or underwriters, or change the program without a formal discussion.

Policy drift rarely happens all at once. A minimum standard becomes slightly more flexible. A vehicle-age limit becomes negotiable. An exception approved for unusual circumstances becomes common. No single decision appears reckless. Together, they create a different program from the one the board approved.

Management should track exception volume, type, approving authority, dealer source, and subsequent performance. The board should review trends rather than waiting for delinquency and losses to confirm that risk increased months or years earlier. Delinquency is a lagging indicator. Exception trends, loan-to-value creep, and dealer concentration are early warning indicators, and they are visible long before a single loan goes bad. These are also the kinds of patterns NCUA's own guidance, cited in Chapter 1, identifies as red flags examiners are trained to look for, which is one more reason exception and concentration data belongs on the board's desk before an exam begins, not after.

- Why are exceptions increasing?
- Which dealers generate them?
- Which underwriters approve them?

- Are the same exceptions recurring?
- Do actual practices still match approved policy?

KEY PRINCIPLE

One exception is judgment. A pattern of exceptions is policy.

Case Study: The Exception That Became Policy

A credit union launches an indirect program with a minimum credit score standard of 680. Three months later, a long-standing dealer submits an applicant at 675. The borrower has stable income, significant time on the job, and otherwise acceptable credit. An exception is approved.

Six months later, another borrower is approved at 672. Nine months later, another is approved at 668. By year-end, management discovers that approximately fifteen percent of approved loans fall below the stated minimum.

Nothing improper occurred at any single step. Each exception appeared reasonable when considered alone. The accumulated decisions, however, created an underwriting standard the board never approved, and a board reviewing only the delinquency report that year would have had no reason to notice.

> **Lesson: When a recurring exception becomes normal practice, management should either restore compliance with the existing standard or bring the proposed change back through the appropriate approval process.**

Automate the Baseline. Underwrite the Exceptions.

A disciplined program should not require an underwriter to analyze every indirect application from the beginning. Well-designed automated decision rules should represent the baseline underwriting standards and quickly identify applications that fit, do not fit, or require judgment.

The baseline rules may consider factors such as the age of the oldest trade line, number of satisfactory trade lines, prior bankruptcy, serious payment delinquencies, accounts currently past due, repossession history, fraud indicators, and other credit-behavior attributes. Credit scores remain useful, but their role may be more effective when used with other variables to establish pricing, maximum loan-to-value, negative-equity limits, and maximum loan amounts rather than as the sole approval standard.

Figure 3-1. Automated approval handles the baseline; human judgment is reserved for true referrals and documented exceptions.

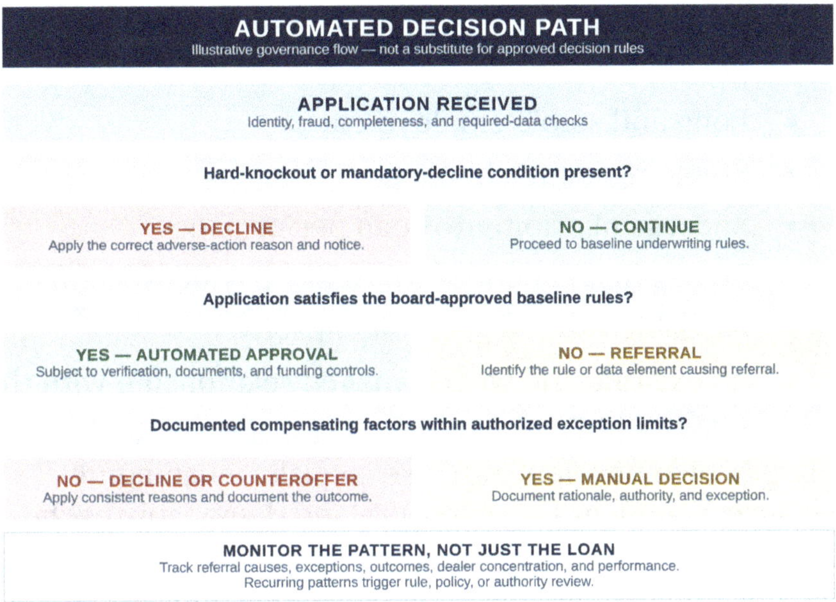

When an application satisfies the baseline rules, an automated approval may be appropriate. When the application receives a referral, the underwriter should focus on the specific rule or rules that were not met and determine whether compensating factors sufficiently reduce the additional risk.

The system should approve applications that fit the underwriting standards. The underwriter's value comes from understanding the exceptions.

Compensating Factors

A referral should not mean "find a way to approve the loan." It should mean "determine whether the strengths of this application reasonably offset the identified weakness." Relevant factors may include:

- A meaningful cash down payment or strong equity position
- Long and stable employment
- Stable residence history
- Successful prior auto-loan performance
- Strong installment or mortgage payment history
- Available revolving-credit capacity
- An existing and well-managed relationship with the credit union

A large down payment can be especially meaningful because it reduces loss exposure and demonstrates the borrower's commitment to the transaction. It should not erase serious credit concerns, but it may reasonably mitigate a marginal exception when the rest of the application is sound.

Case Study: Underwriting the Exception

An application is referred because the borrower has one recent 60-day delinquency. The borrower also has a substantial cash down payment, eight years with the same employer, a long residence history, a previous auto loan paid as agreed, and meaningful available revolving-credit capacity.

The underwriting question is whether the documented strengths sufficiently offset the additional risk created by that delinquency.

> **Lesson: Exception underwriting should evaluate the reason for the referral and the strength of the mitigating factors, not search for a reason to approve the transaction.**

Negative Equity and the Unsecured Portion of the Loan

Negative equity in trade vehicles deserves its own treatment in policy because it is becoming more common, and the dollar amounts are getting larger. A transaction may still fit within the credit union's maximum loan-to-value limit, but that does not mean the structure is sound. When a borrower rolls several thousand dollars of unpaid debt from a prior vehicle into the new loan, the credit union is financing more than the collateral in front of it.

Policy should define the maximum negative equity the credit union is willing to finance, both as a dollar amount and as part of the overall advance limit. It should also define what may offset that exposure. Cash down, manufacturer rebates, dealer discounts, and verified trade equity do not all have the same risk effect. A cash down payment reduces the borrower's financed obligation directly. A rebate may reduce the transaction price, but it does not demonstrate borrower commitment in the same way. A dealer discount may improve the stated structure, but it does not change the fact that prior debt is being carried forward.

Negative equity should also be evaluated before allowing back-end products to be added on top of the transaction. Dealers may expect a lender to approve a loan that includes rolled negative equity and still allow service contracts, GAP, appearance protection, and other aftermarket products above that amount. That is where a loan that technically fits within an LTV limit can become something very different in substance: part secured auto loan and part unsecured loan priced at an auto loan rate.

The board-level standard should be simple: define how much prior debt the credit union is willing to carry into a new vehicle loan, define which offsets count, and decide whether ancillary products may be financed when negative equity is already present. Without that boundary, the maximum LTV becomes a much softer control than it appears.

Automated Declines and Second Looks

Automated decisioning can also improve dealer communication when an application falls materially outside the program's standards. If the maximum allowable loan-to-value is 130 percent and the application requests 145 percent, an immediate decline message may be more useful than allowing the application to sit for hours waiting for a person to reach the same initial conclusion.

The decline does not have to end the discussion. All applications may still receive review, and dealers should have a clear second-look process. Data-entry errors occur. Trade values may be entered incorrectly. Supporting information may be missing. A dealer may restructure the transaction or provide additional information that changes the result.

This approach becomes most valuable during evenings, weekends, holidays, or other periods when a human review may be delayed. Immediate feedback allows the dealer to correct an error, restructure the transaction, or select another lender without unnecessary uncertainty.

The purpose of an automated decline is not to stop the conversation. It is to start the right conversation sooner.

Case Study: Immediate Feedback Produces a Better Result

A dealer submits an application at 145 percent loan-to-value against a maximum standard of 130 percent. The system immediately returns a decline. During the second-look request, the dealer discovers that the trade value was entered incorrectly. After correction, the loan-to-value falls to 126 percent and the application meets the automated approval standards.

> **Lesson: Technology accelerated communication while human review preserved judgment.**

Dealer-Supplied Data, Verified Information, and Handling Misrepresentation

Indirect lending creates an inherent operational tension that direct lending does not: much of the application data originates from an F&I desk whose primary incentive is closing the sale. This is not to suggest that auto dealers are inherently dishonest. Most are running legitimate, highly competitive businesses. However, the dealer's primary objective is completing a transaction today, while the credit union's primary objective is ensuring the loan performs over the next five to seven years. Those goals overlap, but they are far from identical.

That structural misalignment shows up most clearly in dealer-entered demographic data. Ask any veteran loan officer and they will tell you that, according to initial dealer application entries, almost every applicant is a manager, has been at their employer for a decade, and lives nearly rent-free. The system is naturally incentivized toward exaggeration, because stretching income, inflating job tenure, or minimizing housing expenses is often the fastest way to force a system approval through an automated decision engine.

Nationally, this is not just a minor operational headache, it is a systemic industry risk. Point Predictive's 2026 Auto Lending Fraud Trends Report, published April 2026, puts total auto lending fraud exposure, not realized losses, at 10.4 billion dollars for 2025, up from 9.2 billion dollars the year before. Income and employment misrepresentation alone accounts for 45 percent of that exposure and grew 21 percent year over year. If a credit union relies on the initial application fields typed in at the F&I desk to validate repayment capacity, it is underwriting fiction.

The Antidote: Shifting Reliance to Bureau Data and Income Scores

To protect the portfolio without slowing production, a credit union must establish a strict hierarchy of verified information. Unverified application-entry fields should sit at the bottom of that hierarchy. The core underwriting decision should give greater weight to verified, third-party inputs:

- Verified revolving credit capacity and trade line history.

- Credit bureau attributes and address history.
- Automated income-validation scores.
- Fraud and synthetic identity screening tools.

Automated income-validation scores are particularly valuable for credit unions without large underwriting staffs. They allow the credit union to validate affordability and measure requested loan size against verified credit history instantly, without the operational friction and delay of requiring manual pay stubs or W-2s on prime paper.

Managing automated data tools does require real-world calibration. Algorithmic income models are remarkably accurate during stable economic periods, but they inherently lag behind rapid macroeconomic shifts. During periods of high inflation or shifting wage environments, model updates often fall behind actual cost-of-living adjustments and wage growth. A rigid decision engine that enforces a zero-tolerance match between stated income and an income score will repeatedly decline clean, creditworthy paper.

IN PRACTICE

A disciplined program builds in an acceptable tolerance, often a 20 to 30 percent variance between stated application income and the automated income estimate, to account for real-world wage inflation while maintaining a hard boundary against gross misrepresentation.

The Cost of a Stipulation

Relying on bureau data rather than documents affects more than underwriting accuracy. It affects whether the loan reaches the credit union at all. Every stipulation placed on an approval is a point at which the transaction can leave. The dealer has other lenders on the same screen, and at least one of them did not ask.

That matters most in exactly the credit tier this book recommends building a program around. Strong borrowers know they are strong. They expect an approval to reflect what the bureau already shows about them, and they are not inclined to drive home for a pay stub to satisfy a lender they had no relationship with an hour earlier. The dealer, watching a customer's patience run out on a Saturday afternoon, moves the deal. Income-estimation scores exist to solve this problem. They give an underwriter a defensible basis to accept a stated income figure or to question it, and a way to establish affordability without asking a prime borrower to prove something the file already demonstrates.

A credit union that requires income documentation on every loan ends up with less prime paper, not better-performing prime paper. The borrowers willing to tolerate the request are disproportionately the borrowers who had nowhere else to go. A documentation standard adopted to reduce risk can reshape the portfolio toward the applicants it was never meant to attract.

KEY PRINCIPLE

Requiring income verification on every loan does not make prime paper safer. It makes certain there is less of it.

None of this argues for abandoning verification. It argues for spending it where it buys something. Income documentation earns its cost when bureau data and the application disagree beyond the tolerance band, when the credit file is thin enough that the income estimate itself is unreliable, when loan-to-value or payment-to-income already sits at the edge of the standard, when fraud or identity indicators appear, when income is self-employed, commissioned, or otherwise irregular, or when the loan amount exceeds a threshold the board has set. Each of those is a reason management can state out loud. We always ask is not.

Those criteria belong in policy, written down and applied by the same standard to every dealer. This is where a documentation practice stops being an operational preference and becomes a compliance question. A credit union that requires verification on paper and waives it informally for its highest-volume stores has built an unwritten second standard, and Chapter 5 describes what happens when an examiner finds one. Management should track stipulation frequency by credit tier and by dealer alongside look-to-book, which is the measure that shows what the documentation standard is actually costing.

Handling Misrepresentation: The Mindset

Every indirect program will eventually catch a deal where the application numbers do not align with the hard data. How the underwriting team handles those moments determines whether the credit union maintains control of its underwriting standards or burns its dealer network.

An underwriter who takes a dealer's misrepresentation personally, treating a data mismatch as an insult rather than a data problem, is bringing the wrong mindset to a fast-moving, transactional business. Taking bad data personally creates friction, damages relationships, and leads to unproductive confrontation.

The objective when confronting bad data is simple: decline or restructure the bad paper without damaging the dealer relationship. The tactic is to separate the F&I manager from the misrepresentation entirely.

> KEY PRINCIPLE
>
> **Never accuse the dealer of lying. Frame every data discrepancy as a mismatch between the borrower's stated claims and the verified bureau data.**

The specific language an underwriter uses matters less than the discipline behind it: acknowledge the intent to help fund the deal, state plainly that the numbers do not reconcile with verified data, and let the borrower's documentation, not the dealer's word, close the gap. A standardized version of that conversation belongs in underwriting training material, not in a strategy chapter, but every CEO approving an indirect program should confirm one exists and that staff are using it consistently.

Done well, this approach preserves the dealer relationship by placing responsibility for the discrepancy on the applicant rather than the dealer, establishes that the credit union underwrites to verified data rather than to whatever a system override allows, and filters paper naturally. A dealer who intentionally inflated the numbers tends to move the deal to a less disciplined lender. A dealer with a legitimate deal works with the borrower to close the gap.

Case Study: Underwriting the Data Mismatch

A dealer submits an application for a prime borrower showing $9,500 in monthly income and $500 in housing expenses. The borrower is requesting a 125 percent loan-to-value advance on a used vehicle.

The credit union's automated income-estimation score indicates an estimated income closer to $5,200 per month, well outside the acceptable tolerance band. Credit bureau trade lines also show a long-standing mortgage payment of $1,800 per month, directly contradicting the $500 in housing expense typed into the aggregator platform.

Instead of issuing an immediate flat decline or accusing the F&I desk of inflating the file to force an approval, the underwriter first recalculates the borrower's capacity using the income estimate rather than the stated income. If the recalculated capacity remains within policy, the credit union may be able to approve the loan without further documentation. If it falls outside policy at the requested structure, the loan officer calls the F&I manager and explains, without accusation, that the verified bureau capacity and housing obligations support approval at 105 percent loan-to-value, or that documentation would be needed to validate the higher claimed income and support the requested 125 percent advance.

The dealer realizes the credit union is underwriting the verified bureau file rather than the application entry screen. Two hours later, the dealer restructures the transaction with an additional $3,000 in cash down from the buyer, bringing the advance within the 105 percent requirement, and the loan funds safely.

> **Lesson: Holding firm on verified inputs while delivering the message professionally protected the credit union's collateral position and still let the dealer complete the sale.**

Ancillary Products, Member Protection, and Transaction Quality

Credit policy should consider more than repayment probability. It should also address collateral exposure, reputation risk, member treatment, and overall transaction quality.

Dealers often discuss "front-end" and "back-end" products as if they were separate from the lender's perspective. They are not. The borrower signs one obligation, and the credit union finances one transaction. Products such as service contracts, GAP coverage, maintenance plans, tire protection, paint and fabric protection, dent protection, and theft-recovery products all increase the balance the borrower must repay.

Some products may provide legitimate value to a borrower. That does not mean every amount should be financed. Even products described as refundable may provide little meaningful value to the credit union two or three years later when a default occurs. The board may reasonably establish a dollar limit, percentage limit, or both, with clearly defined exception authority.

Case Study: The $8,000 Ancillary Product Package

A borrower purchases a used vehicle for $24,000. The transaction includes a vehicle service contract, GAP coverage, tire and wheel coverage, paint protection, and fabric protection. The ancillary products total more than $8,000.

The borrower qualifies, the credit score is strong, and the disclosures appear complete. The deal structure shows the borrower actually arrived with $20,000 available for the purchase. Rather than applying most of those funds toward vehicle equity, the transaction was structured to route a substantial share of it into the ancillary product package instead, leaving the loan itself larger and more thinly secured than the borrower's own cash would have allowed.

A lender focused only on approval metrics may approve the structure as submitted. A lender focused on transaction quality has to separately decide whether that structure aligns with its standards, mission, and reputation-risk tolerance, regardless of how strong the borrower's credit looks on paper.

> **Lesson: Credit quality alone does not make every transaction structure appropriate. A large down payment is only a meaningful compensating factor if it actually reaches the loan, not the ancillary product package.**

Borrower Understanding and Consistent Treatment

Some consumers may have limited experience with complex vehicle-finance products or may depend heavily on the dealer's explanation of the transaction. A credit union may not be able to determine whether a borrower fully understood every product or whether pressure occurred at the point of sale. Policy can nevertheless establish neutral, consistently applied limits that reduce the likelihood of participating in transactions that create a strong appearance of consumer harm.

These safeguards should be based on the structure of the transaction and applied consistently, not on assumptions about an individual borrower. Clear limits protect the borrower, the credit union, and the integrity of the program.

A credit union's job is not to decide what a dealer may sell. Its job is to decide which transactions it is willing to participate in.

The Holder Rule as a Policy Boundary

Chapter 1 introduced the Holder Rule and its liability exposure; this section applies it at the policy level. Indirect lending connects the credit union to more than the borrower's promise to repay. Under the Federal Trade Commission's Holder Rule, a consumer credit contract preserves the consumer's ability to assert against a purchaser of the contract the claims and defenses the consumer could assert against the seller. That makes dealer conduct and transaction quality relevant to the lender, even when the lender did not make the original sales representations.

Not every dealer dispute becomes lender liability, and the precise result depends on the facts and applicable law. Still, management should not view the purchased contract as isolated from the underlying sale. Dealer due diligence, transaction controls, complaint monitoring, and legal review belong in the program design. Chapter 5 addresses the compliance and legal framework in greater detail.

Before approving any transaction structure, management and the board should be able to answer a simple test: would we be comfortable explaining why we participated in this transaction to our board, regulator, examiner, or member advocate? A transaction that fails that test deserves a second look regardless of how well the borrower qualifies.

The Lines We Will Not Cross

Policy defines what a program is allowed to become. The most useful board conversation before adopting it starts from a single statement: just because we can make a loan does not mean we should.

That conversation should produce three short lists. Transaction characteristics that would cause concern regardless of how well the borrower qualifies. Exception patterns that would require management action or board review. Indicators that would suggest the program is drifting from its intended purpose. Three of each is enough. A board that cannot name three in any category has not yet formed a view on where its limits are.

Compare those answers against the proposed policy. A concern the board identifies but the policy does not reflect should either be accepted deliberately or written into the framework. Leaving it in neither place is how a boundary quietly becomes an assumption.

The Board Exercise, a separate companion document, runs this as its own forty-five-minute session, available with the other companion materials at https://mycurisk.com/volume.

Things That Get Credit Unions Into Trouble

The governance failures behind most troubled indirect programs are rarely dramatic. They are small, cumulative, and easy to justify one at a time:

- Writing operating procedure into board policy instead of keeping policy at the boundary level.
- Allowing exceptions to accumulate without tracking volume, source, approving authority, or performance.
- Reviewing only delinquency at the board level and missing earlier indicators like exception trends, loan-to-value creep, and dealer concentration.
- Treating dealer-supplied information as sufficient without an independent verification hierarchy.

- Financing ancillary products without a defined dollar or percentage limit and clear exception authority.
- Structuring transactions to route a borrower's cash away from loan equity and into ancillary products without noticing the effect on the credit union's actual collateral position.
- Building board and regulatory reporting after volume has already arrived instead of before launch.
- Treating every dealer data discrepancy as a personal dispute rather than a routine file-level clarification.
- Requiring income documentation on every loan without measuring what the requirement costs in funded prime volume.
- Applying income-verification requirements inconsistently across dealers, so that the documented standard and the actual practice no longer match.

Individually, each of these looks like a minor operational choice. Together, they produce a program the board never actually approved.

Chapter Summary

- The board's role is to define acceptable risk. Management's role is to convert that risk appetite into underwriting standards, automated decision rules, procedures, and reporting that can be executed consistently.

- Credit unions do not have to develop automated decision rules from internal experience alone. Credit bureaus, analytics firms, consultants, and LOS implementation teams can help translate board-approved risk appetite into executable decision rules, but management remains responsible for ensuring those rules fit the credit union's policy, technology, and actual portfolio performance.
- The strongest program automates routine decisions, directs human judgment toward true exceptions, monitors how often those exceptions occur, and acts before temporary accommodations become an unofficial policy.
- Delinquency is a lagging indicator. Exception trends, loan-to-value creep, and dealer concentration are early warning indicators the board should review directly, not wait to have confirmed by losses.
- Dealer-supplied data has value but should never be the sole basis for a decision. Verification is about better information, not distrust.
- Credit discipline includes transaction discipline. A legally permissible sale is not automatically a transaction the credit union must finance, and ancillary product limits protect the credit union's collateral position as much as the member.
- The institution should decide in advance what it is willing to participate in, apply those limits consistently, and remain prepared to explain those decisions to its board, members, and regulators.

- Verification has a price. Every stipulation is a point at which a dealer can move the transaction to a lender that did not ask, and in prime credit that risk is real. Income-estimation scores exist so a credit union can establish affordability without paying that price on every file.
- The circumstances requiring income documentation should be defined in policy and applied consistently. A verification standard that exists on paper but is waived informally for high-volume dealers is both policy drift and a fair lending exposure.

Board Discussion Questions

The full version of these questions lives in the Board and Management Discussion Guide, the companion document for this chapter, available at https://mycurisk.com/volume. The following are the core governance questions.

1. What risks are we unwilling to accept regardless of loan-growth opportunities?
2. What exception level or pattern would cause us to reconsider the program's underwriting standards?
3. What transaction structures would make us uncomfortable even when the borrower qualifies?
4. What ancillary-product limits are consistent with our mission, collateral exposure, and reputation-risk tolerance?
5. How will we know whether actual practices are drifting from the policy we approved?

6. What reports would our regulator expect management and the board to produce and review if the program were examined tomorrow?
7. Under what circumstances do we require income documentation, and can we state a reason for each one beyond habit?
8. Do we know what our verification requirements cost us in funded volume, and are they applied the same way for every dealer?

CEO Action Items

The detailed implementation checklist is part of the same Board and Management Discussion Guide, and the underwriting standards and limits it produces should be tested against the Indirect Lending Risk Assessment, both available at https://mycurisk.com/volume. Before launch, the CEO should ensure that management has completed these core actions.

1. **Separate policy from procedure:** ensure board policy establishes boundaries while procedures govern operations.
2. **Validate the decision-rule framework:** confirm that any automated underwriting rules were developed using appropriate internal data, outside expertise, or both, and that the LOS or decision engine can actually execute the rules as intended.
3. **Establish exception tracking:** begin monitoring exception volume and reporting before the first loan is funded.

4. **Define the data hierarchy:** establish the hierarchy of verified data and the second-look process.
5. **Set ancillary-product limits:** establish ancillary-product and transaction-quality limits.
6. **Build reporting before launch:** establish board and regulatory reporting before volume arrives.
7. **Define the verification triggers:** specify in policy when income documentation is required, and confirm each trigger can be justified by something other than practice.
8. **Measure what verification costs:** track stipulation frequency and look-to-book by credit tier and by dealer.

Chapter 4: Technology Infrastructure

Where Strategy Meets Dealer Speed

A credit union can have strong governance, sound underwriting standards, and experienced staff, yet still struggle in indirect lending if its technology environment cannot consistently execute what management and the board approved. Technology does not create strategy. It determines whether strategy can be executed at dealer speed. Indirect lending occurs at the point of sale, where dealers expect quick responses and reliable funding. Technology is the bridge between board-approved underwriting standards and the dealer experience.

A vendor demonstration is built to show a system working well, not to show where it runs into a credit union's specific underwriting logic. That gap tends to surface after the contract is signed, not before, which is exactly why this chapter exists before Chapter 7's dealer launch rather than after it.

Is This an Indirect Lending Project, or Also an LOS Project?

Before evaluating a single vendor, a credit union needs an honest answer to a more basic question. Can the core and loan origination system already in place actually support an indirect lending program, or does building this program also mean replacing or materially upgrading the LOS at the same time?

Many credit unions approach indirect lending as an add-on to systems chosen years earlier for a different volume and a different workflow. A core or LOS built around low-volume direct lending and manual underwriting may lack the real-time decisioning, dealer connectivity, or data-field flexibility indirect lending requires. The earlier decision was reasonable at the time; the mismatch had no reason to surface until now.

This should be confirmed early, not discovered midway through a dealer rollout. If the honest answer is that the current core or LOS cannot reasonably support the program, management and the board are no longer looking at one project. They are looking at two, an indirect lending program, and a core or LOS replacement or upgrade that has to happen first or alongside it. Naming that reality early changes the timeline, the budget, and the sequence of decisions still ahead. It does not change whether indirect lending remains the right strategic decision, only how much work stands between that decision and a dealer's first application.

How the Borrower Will Actually Pay You

The core and LOS question has a smaller companion that credit unions routinely discover after launch. An indirect borrower is a member on paper. The checking account the payment will come from is almost certainly somewhere else, and financing a vehicle is not going to move it. Direct lending never forced this question, because the borrower was usually already banking with the credit union before the loan existed.

Those borrowers arrive expecting to pay the way they pay everyone else. Most will ask for a debit card option. ACH from an external account works as well and costs the credit union considerably less, and a recurring ACH authorization captured at booking is the strongest control available over first-payment performance. A pay-by-phone or agent-assisted channel is worth having for the borrower who will use neither.

The selection question is which option integrates cleanly with the core and posts in real time, whatever the length of its feature list. A payment portal that batches overnight generates a service call every time a borrower pays on the due date and then sees a late fee, and those calls arrive at a relationship with no branch history to fall back on.

Timing matters as much as the channel. If the account is not payable for several days after booking, the welcome packet arrives promising a method that does not yet work. Chapter 8 treats an early payment default as a signal worth investigating at the dealer level, and it is. But a program that cannot accept a payment on the day it told the borrower to make one will generate first-payment problems of its own and then read them as someone else's.

Two decisions inside this should be made deliberately rather than by default. The first is whether to charge a fee for debit or card payments. Fees of this kind have drawn regulatory and litigation attention, and the answer belongs with counsel rather than with the operations budget. The second is that a payment provider is a vendor. It holds member data, it can go down, and it belongs in the same due diligence, information-security review, and business continuity plan as the aggregator and the loan origination system.

None of this has to be solved before deciding whether indirect lending fits the credit union's strategy. It is a dependency that should be named during the core and LOS conversation rather than discovered by the first borrower who tries to make a payment.

Technology Should Support Policy, Not Replace It

Underwriting standards should drive system configuration, not the other way around. In reality, every decision engine has limitations. Data-field availability, custom calculation restrictions, and platform constraints can prevent technology from implementing underwriting standards exactly as written. When that happens, find a different way to achieve the same risk objective rather than abandoning the standard.

> KEY PRINCIPLE
>
> **A system outage is only the obvious technology risk. The quieter risk is assuming the decision engine, LOS, or integration can enforce a control that it cannot actually calculate, read, or route.**

Case Study: The Income Score Problem

A credit union wanted to strengthen its indirect underwriting program by comparing an income-estimation score against both the borrower's stated income and the amount being financed. The concept was straightforward. If a borrower claimed substantially more income than the estimate suggested, and was requesting a high loan amount, the application should receive additional review.

The problem appeared during implementation. The decision engine could evaluate minimum and maximum values and compare data fields to fixed limits. What it could not do was perform the exact calculation management had written into the underwriting standards. The vendor demonstrated several alternative approaches, but none duplicated the formula exactly.

The easiest solution would have been to remove the control entirely. The implementation team resisted that temptation. Instead, management analyzed historical applications and built a series of decision bands. Applications falling within normal income-estimation ranges continued through automated underwriting. Applications showing progressively larger differences between stated income, estimated income, and requested loan amount were routed into review queues with escalating levels of scrutiny. For example, an income-estimation score of 0060, indicating roughly $60,000 in annual income, paired with a stated income above $80,000, would trigger a manual review. Ideally, the score could also be used to calculate an alternate debt-to-income figure, but the system does not support that calculation directly.

The final configuration required more rules than originally anticipated, but the underlying risk control remained intact. Six months after launch, management reviewed the referrals those rules had generated. Several applications would have been approved under the original automated workflow because stated income greatly exceeded what the borrower actually earned. The workaround was imperfect, but it did what the original rule was intended to do.

> **Lesson: Technology limitations do not eliminate risk. Management's responsibility is to find another way to achieve the same control objective, not to abandon the objective because implementing it is inconvenient.**

Credit Score Options for Your Indirect Program

A wide range of primary credit scores are available to build an indirect lending program around. Some are general-purpose scores that apply to any type of credit application. Others are modeled specifically to be predictive for a particular loan type, such as auto or credit card lending. Within either category, there are usually two or three sub-models in circulation at any given time, based on the year each version was released.

For an indirect lending program, an auto-enhanced credit score is the stronger choice over a general-purpose score, since it is built specifically to predict how a borrower is likely to perform on this kind of credit rather than credit in general. Within that auto-enhanced category, favor the sub-model that is well established and already in common use by the dealers in your market. All three major credit bureaus offer comparable auto-enhanced score models, so the practical decision is less about which bureau and more about which sub-model your target dealers and their aggregator platforms are already built around.

There is a second, more practical reason to favor the model your dealers already use, beyond workflow convenience. A dealer typically pulls scores from all three bureaus and shops the loan across several lenders and their decision engines. If a credit union underwrites on a score model that happens to rate a given borrower more favorably than the sub-models the rest of the market is using on that same file, the credit union tends to win exactly the applications where its own score was the outlier. A less common or lower-cost score is not inherently riskier on its own terms. In practice, though, it can produce adverse selection: a "top-tier" portfolio that is, on average, riskier than the tier label suggests, because it is disproportionately built from borrowers whose other bureau scores rated them a tier lower. I have seen this pattern firsthand; test it against your own approved population rather than assuming an unusual score choice is free.

If your loan origination system and dealer network both support multiple score models, configure more than the credit score alone. An income-estimation score is a strong addition, and a debt-to-income figure is worth at least considering. Each of these three, the credit score, the income estimate, and the debt-to-income figure, is a reference point that speaks to a borrower's willingness and capacity to repay beyond what was presented on the application itself. None of them replaces underwriting judgment, but together they give an underwriter and a decision engine more to work with than a single score in isolation.

Whichever model you settle on, avoid building the choice around a single bureau's coverage.

Dealer Submission Platforms and Loan Origination Systems

Indirect lending relies on multiple systems. Dealer submission platforms focus on dealer convenience and lender selection. Loan origination systems focus on lender controls, auditability, and compliance. Friction occurs at the connection point. Every manual touchpoint introduces delay, cost, or inconsistency. Successful programs spend considerable effort eliminating unnecessary handoffs while preserving human judgment where it adds value.

The dealer-facing network and the lender's loan origination system are built for different customers, and that distinction matters. A dealer network's priorities center on the dealer's experience: one data-entry point, access to many competing lenders, fast status updates, and predictable funding. A loan origination system exists for a different purpose: consistent underwriting, credit bureau and identity verification, exception controls and audit trails, and accurate funding and core boarding. Selecting a strong system on one side does not guarantee the other side is solved. A credit union should design around its target dealers' actual workflow first, then work backward into its own systems and controls.

Chapter 1 named CUDL, RouteOne, and Dealertrack as examples of dealer submission platforms; this section covers what actually differentiates them. CUDL, operated by the credit union service organization Origence, is built specifically around the credit union channel. RouteOne, founded by several major captive finance companies, is used broadly across banks, captives, and credit unions, and is often the platform a franchise dealer is already using regardless of who ends up financing the deal. Dealertrack, a Cox Automotive brand, offers similarly broad reach along with deeper integration into other Cox dealer systems for dealers already committed to that ecosystem. None of these is automatically the right choice. The more useful question is which platform the credit union's actual target dealers already use as their primary portal, since a credit union's own preference matters far less than a dealer's daily habit.

On the loan origination side, MeridianLink, nCino, Origence's own arcOS platform, and Jack Henry's LoanVantage are among the systems credit unions commonly use to manage indirect underwriting, documentation, and funding. Each connects to the major dealer networks in some fashion, and each markets automated decisioning, verification tools, and reporting capability. Exactly how deep that connectivity runs, and which features are native versus requiring additional configuration or cost, changes often enough that it should be confirmed directly against current vendor materials and existing customer references rather than assumed from a features list.

Whether an LOS connects to CUDL, RouteOne, or Dealertrack is only the starting point. The better due-diligence question is what data, decisions, documents, and funding information actually move in each direction, how quickly they move, and what an employee has to do manually when that transfer fails.

Fully In-House Origination

A small number of credit unions build an indirect program without a dealer network or a commercial LOS at all, running everything through individual dealer agreements and a manual or internally built application path. This is technically possible, and a handful of credit unions have done it. This book does not cover that approach beyond acknowledging that it exists. This is generally not the recommended path, outside of a program led by someone with deep, direct indirect lending experience who has already chosen it deliberately. A credit union in a position to do that successfully is not the credit union this book is written for.

Selecting a Vendor Combination: What the Evaluation Should Actually Test

Most vendor evaluations compare feature lists, pricing, and reference calls. Those matter, but they rarely reveal how a system behaves against a credit union's actual underwriting standards, and a features list can make two very different products look identical on paper.

A more useful evaluation asks a vendor to demonstrate the specific scenarios that matter most: an applicant just below the credit-score floor with strong compensating factors, a Saturday afternoon volume spike, a trade-value mismatch between systems, a borrower who needs to be declined immediately rather than left waiting. A vendor that can only speak in generalities about these scenarios during the sales process is unlikely to handle them any better after the contract is signed.

Case Study: The RFP That Asked the Wrong Questions

A credit union preparing for an indirect lending launch issued a request for proposal to several loan origination and decision-engine vendors.

The evaluation committee built a traditional scoring matrix. Questions focused on implementation cost, annual licensing fees, uptime statistics, support hours, and the number of advertised features. Vendor responses were impressive. Every system offered automated underwriting, dealer connectivity, credit bureau integration, document generation, and reporting. One vendor scored highest while also representing the lowest overall cost, and the credit union signed with them.

Six months later, implementation was underway when a significant problem surfaced. The credit union's underwriting standards set a maximum dollar amount a dealer could add to a loan through aftermarket products, service contracts, and other add-on sales. During implementation, the team discovered the system had no way to aggregate the individual aftermarket line items into a single total. Loans could be approved that exceeded the board-established limit without the system ever flagging it, the exact ancillary product exposure Chapter 3 warns against.

Looking back, management realized the RFP never asked a vendor to demonstrate how loan policy guidelines were actually enforced in the decision process. Had the RFP required vendors to walk through five or ten representative applications, including approvals, declines, stipulations, exceptions, and dealer-submitted corrections, the limitation would have surfaced before the contract was signed instead of six months into implementation.

The vendor had not misrepresented the product. The credit union had simply asked the wrong questions, and now had to build a manual workaround to estimate aggregate ancillary exposure until the system could be reconfigured.

> **Lesson: An RFP built around features identifies what a vendor can sell. An RFP built around real underwriting scenarios reveals how the system performs in the situations that actually matter.**

Automating Workflow, Routing the Exceptions

Chapter 3 established which decisions should be automated and which should be referred for underwriting judgment. This section covers the operational side of that same line: routine approvals, routine declines, bureau retrieval, fraud screening, and income estimation should generally be automated. Human review should focus on situations where context matters. Technology should identify exceptions. Underwriters should understand them.

When Human Review Matters

Good decision engines frequently refer thin credit files, limited trade histories, prior bankruptcies, non-spousal co-borrowers, existing member relationships, and transactions involving large negative trades. These are not necessarily weak loans. They are loans that require context. A borrower with two years of perfect mortgage history and a meaningful down payment may present less risk than a bureau score alone suggests. Technology can identify the file. A human has to evaluate the story.

The Weekend Problem

Dealers sell vehicles when members are available, not when lender offices are staffed. Saturday afternoons, evenings, and holiday weekends expose weaknesses in both systems and workflow design. Technology should answer two simple questions. Who knows an application arrived? How quickly can someone respond?

A good decision engine reduces urgency on most loans by resolving them automatically. For a program that wants to compete on service, that is not quite enough on its own. A workable standard for many programs is at least one pass through the loan queue in the evening, roughly six to eight o'clock, and at least two passes on Saturday and Sunday, commonly in the two to four o'clock and six to eight o'clock windows. What your program can actually support depends on staffing, but consider a dedicated phone line dealers can call with questions, monitored more closely than a standard business-hours line. Larger lenders often keep loan officers reachable by cell phone during their review windows for exactly this reason, and a credit union competing for the same dealer's attention should at least weigh whether it can do the same on a scale it can sustain.

Case Study: The Saturday Approval That Wasn't

A dealer submitted an application at 2:15 p.m. on a Saturday. The credit union's automated underwriting system approved the loan within thirty seconds. From the credit union's perspective, the transaction was complete. From the dealer's perspective, it was not.

The dealer still needed clarification on an income stipulation the decision engine had generated. No loan officer was scheduled to review referrals until Monday morning. By then, the dealer had already assigned the deal to another lender that had not stipulated for income documentation at all.

When management reviewed the event, they initially treated it as a dealer-relations issue. The real cause turned out to be a technology and workflow mismatch. The system had approved the credit decision exactly as configured. What it had not done was provide any practical way to resolve a follow-up question during the dealer's actual operating hours.

Afterward, management began tracking both automated decision time and final decision time, the point at which stipulations and conditions are actually cleared. The second metric turned out to be a far more accurate picture of the dealer's real experience than the first.

> **Lesson: Dealers do not measure how quickly a credit union approves a loan. They measure how quickly a transaction reaches a funded conclusion.**

Some programs address weekend and evening capacity by using a third-party underwriting service rather than expanding internal staff hours. This can be a reasonable way to extend coverage, with one caution. A third party should apply the credit union's guidelines, not make exceptions to them. If you use an outsourced underwriting provider, every exception it approves should be reviewed during normal business hours, and the credit union should give the provider ongoing feedback so its decisions stay aligned with actual program performance rather than drifting on their own. Do not rely on faith. Verify. Chapter 6 covers this same boundary in more depth, since it applies just as much to a dealer relationship manager as it does to an underwriting vendor.

Integration Friction and the False Decline

Many indirect lending delays are not credit problems. They are integration problems. Gross versus net income fields, housing-expense categories, trade values, negative-equity calculations, dealer incentives, and borrower data can all be interpreted differently by connected systems. A clean application may become a referral because of data translation rather than risk.

Technology can create unintended consequences of its own. An incorrectly mapped field, incomplete information, or vendor outage may generate a decline that would otherwise be approved. Strong programs maintain second-look processes because technology should accelerate communication, not eliminate accountability.

This is why every integration should be tested with real or realistic application examples before launch. Management should know which fields drive automated decisions, which fields require manual confirmation, and which errors create referrals that look like credit judgment but are really system translation issues.

Figure 4-1. Indirect lending depends on reliable handoffs from dealer submission through servicing and monitoring.

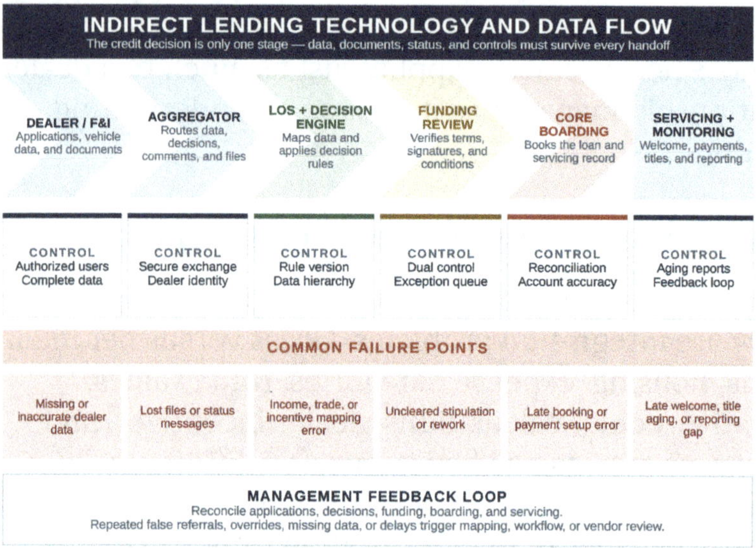

Case Study: The Good Loan That Became a Refer

A transaction meets every material underwriting standard. Because a trade value maps incorrectly between systems, the loan is referred for manual review instead of approved automatically. The underwriter approves it without difficulty. The borrower still receives financing, but the dealer experiences hours of unnecessary delay for a loan that was never actually in question.

> **Lesson: The problem was not credit quality. The problem was technology friction, and it was invisible to anyone who only looked at the final decision.**

Choosing Manual Workarounds Deliberately

Technology debt often appears as spreadsheets, duplicate data entry, manual reconciliations, and temporary workarounds. Many credit unions build practical solutions that solve immediate problems, and there is nothing wrong with that on its own. The risk lies in building one without deciding, at the moment you build it, who owns it, why it exists, and when you will revisit it.

If a manual process is the right call for now, document that decision the same way you would document a policy exception. Name an owner. Write down the specific problem it solves and the volume or condition under which you expect to replace it with something more permanent. Revisit that decision on a schedule rather than waiting for the workaround to become load-bearing enough that nobody wants to touch it.

KEY PRINCIPLE

Temporary solutions have a habit of becoming permanent. A workaround that solves this month's problem is still a workaround, even after it has been running for three years.

Vendor Management

Governance does not stop when the vendor contract is signed. Management should evaluate service-level agreements, escalation procedures, outage notifications, status pages, support responsiveness, weekend coverage, and 24/7 support options. Technology relationships require the same ongoing oversight as dealer relationships, not a one-time review during procurement.

A vendor's sales team will say yes to almost anything during a demo. Whether the system can actually do a specific thing, inside the credit union's specific underwriting standards, at dealer speed, on a Saturday afternoon, usually only becomes clear during implementation. Building the evaluation questions from the earlier section in this chapter into the RFP process is what surfaces that gap before the contract is signed instead of after.

Business Continuity and Concentration Risk

Many institutions depend on a single bureau provider, decision engine, or loan origination system. At a minimum, management should consider maintaining a secondary bureau relationship. Secondary bureau access is useful during outages and when a borrower has frozen a particular bureau file, a situation that otherwise stops an application cold regardless of how strong the underwriting is. Beyond disaster recovery, a backup provider offers operational flexibility that pays for itself the first time the primary system is unavailable during business hours.

Technology Decisions Require Ongoing Review

Decision rules, integrations, data mapping logic, and workflow assumptions should be reviewed periodically. Fraud patterns change. Dealer behavior changes. Portfolio performance changes. Technology governance is the operational equivalent of policy governance, covered in Chapter 3. Failure to review technology eventually creates the technical equivalent of policy drift, a system still enforcing rules nobody re-examined since launch.

Things That Get Credit Unions Into Trouble

Technology failures in an indirect program rarely look like a system outage. They look like these:

- Assuming the existing core and LOS can support indirect lending volume without confirming it first.
- Buying technology before defining underwriting standards.
- Excessive manual workarounds that never get formalized or replaced.
- Poor data mapping between the dealer submission platform and the loan origination system.
- Over-automating judgment that requires human context.
- Under-automating routine work that a decision engine could handle reliably.

- Vendor dependence without a contingency plan for an outage or a frozen bureau file.
- Building solutions more complex than actual volume requires.
- Ignoring technology controls once implementation is complete, instead of reviewing them on a schedule.
- Assuming a borrower who banks somewhere else will find a way to pay you.
- Selecting a payment channel on price or features without confirming it posts to the core in real time.

None of these failures start as a crisis. They start as a reasonable-sounding shortcut, a manual workaround nobody circled back to formalize or an automation decision nobody revisited as volume changed, and over time the technology stops matching the program it was built to support.

Chapter Summary

- Confirm early whether the existing core and LOS can actually support indirect lending. If they cannot, this is two projects, a lending program and a system replacement or upgrade, not one.
- Technology is an execution tool. Underwriting standards should drive system configuration, not the other way around.
- When a system cannot implement a standard exactly as written, rebuild the control inside the

system's actual capabilities rather than dropping the standard.

- Automate routine approvals, declines, and data retrieval. Reserve human judgment for the files that require context, thin files, prior bankruptcies, large down payments, existing member relationships.
- The weekend and holiday workflow is where technology gaps show up first, because that is when dealers need an answer and lender offices are least staffed.
- Integration friction, not credit risk, causes many of the delays and false declines in indirect lending. Maintain a second-look process for exactly this reason.
- Temporary workarounds become permanent infrastructure if nobody decides otherwise. Track technology debt the same way exception volume is tracked in Chapter 3.
- Vendor oversight does not end at contract signing, and a vendor evaluation built around specific underwriting scenarios reveals more than one built around price and feature counts.
- A single point of failure (one bureau, one decision engine, one origination system) is a concentration risk. Review technology decisions on a schedule, the same way policy is reviewed.
- An indirect borrower's primary checking account is almost never at the credit union. Confirm how that borrower will actually make a payment, how quickly it posts, and how soon after booking the

channel works, before launch rather than after the first welcome packet goes out.

Board Discussion Questions

1. Have we confirmed our current core and LOS can actually support this program, or are we already looking at two projects instead of one?
2. Does our technology support the underwriting standards we approved, or has it quietly begun to shape them?
3. Where are we dependent on manual processing, and what happens to that step if the person doing it is unavailable?
4. What would happen to our indirect program if a critical vendor became unavailable tomorrow?
5. How would we know if technology were overriding policy rather than executing it?
6. Can our current systems support the volume growth we are projecting, or only the volume we have today?
7. What technology decisions has management made that the board has never actually reviewed?
8. How will an indirect borrower who does not bank with us make a payment, what does that channel cost us, and have we decided deliberately whether to pass any of it on?

CEO Action Items

1. **Confirm core and LOS capability first:** before evaluating dealer networks or new vendors, determine whether the current core and LOS can support indirect lending as designed, or whether this is now also a core or LOS project.
2. **Map every system involved in indirect lending:** document the dealer submission platform, decision engine, loan origination system, and every connection point between them.
3. **Identify manual bottlenecks:** find every place a person, not a system, is currently the reason an application waits.
4. **Define acceptable decision and funding timelines:** set a specific standard for both, and measure actual performance against it.
5. **Test weekend and holiday workflows deliberately:** do not wait for an actual Saturday afternoon volume spike to discover a gap.
6. **Review vendor resiliency and maintain contingency plans:** including a secondary bureau relationship where appropriate.
7. **Build a scenario-based vendor evaluation framework:** require prospective vendors to demonstrate specific underwriting scenarios before any contract is signed, not just a general product demo.
8. **Confirm the payment path before launch:** determine which payment channels an indirect borrower will have, whether they post to the core

in real time, how soon after booking they work, and who owns the vendor relationship behind them.

Chapter 5: Compliance and Legal Review

You Inherit the Dealer's Transaction

By the time a credit union reaches this chapter, it has already defined a strategy, evaluated whether a realistic market opportunity exists, established board-approved boundaries, and examined whether its technology can execute those boundaries consistently. At this point, many institutions believe the difficult work is finished. It is not.

Compliance and legal review are often treated as final checks shortly before launch. In indirect lending, they need to shape the program much earlier: dealer agreements, system configuration, compensation structure, documentation standards, exception authority, complaint monitoring, and geographic scope should all reflect the compliance framework before the first contract is purchased.

The credit union did not negotiate the vehicle price. It did not present every ancillary product. It may not have prepared the retail installment contract. Yet it is purchasing the contract, placing the loan on its books, communicating with the member, and inheriting exposure connected to the underlying transaction. That makes compliance a program-design responsibility, not a file-review responsibility.

This chapter will not turn a CEO or board member into legal counsel, but it should help leadership ask the right questions, assign responsibility clearly, and build evidence that the program is operating as approved. The strongest indirect programs do not wait for an examiner, attorney, or member complaint to reveal how the process actually works.

Compliance Is a Governance Issue

Boards do not need to interpret every provision of Regulation Z, Regulation B, the Equal Credit Opportunity Act, the Military Lending Act, or state retail installment sales laws. They do need reasonable assurance that management identifies the rules that apply, translates them into controls, tests those controls, and reports when actual practice begins to drift.

Most serious compliance failures do not begin with an intentional decision to violate a rule. They begin with an assumption. Management assumes the dealer sent the notice. The dealer assumes the lender sent it. The vendor says the system can enforce a limit, but nobody tests the actual transaction. A contract provision allows a chargeback, but the credit union never invokes it. Each assumption looks small until a pattern develops.

From a governance perspective, the useful question is rarely, "Who made the mistake?" The better question is, "What control allowed the mistake to become a pattern?" One defective file may be an error. Repeated defects indicate a process problem. A process problem left uncorrected becomes a governance problem.

The Three Questions Every Transaction Must Pass

Many lenders ask one question: can we buy this loan? A disciplined program asks three. Is the transaction legally permissible? Does it comply with the credit union's policy, underwriting standards, and operating controls? And is it a transaction the credit union is willing to participate in when member treatment, collateral exposure, and reputation risk are considered?

Figure 5-1. A transaction must pass legal, institutional, and governance review before the credit union participates.

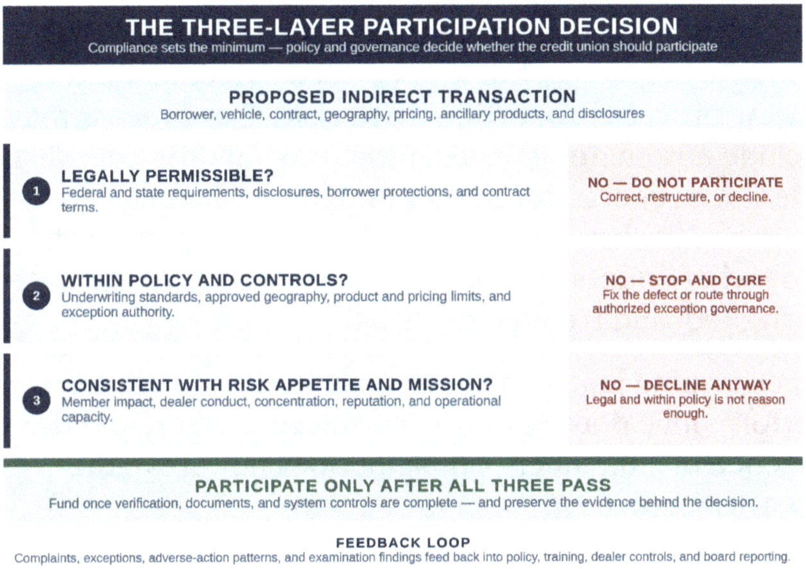

These tests are not interchangeable. A transaction may be legal and still fall outside the institution's standards. It may satisfy underwriting requirements and still reveal poor transaction quality.

KEY PRINCIPLE

Compliance sets the floor. Governance decides whether the credit union should own the transaction after member treatment, collateral exposure, dealer conduct, and reputation risk are considered.

Regulation Z: More Than APR Accuracy

Regulation Z is commonly reduced to APR, finance charge, payment, and disclosure accuracy. Those items matter, but the board-level issue is broader: what process gives management confidence that purchased contracts are accurate before funds leave the credit union?

A credit union need not rebuild every dealer contract from the beginning, but it does need a documented review process proportionate to risk. That process may include automated recalculation, pre-funding checklists, tolerance reports, targeted sampling, and enhanced review of dealers with repeated defects. Whatever the tool, what counts is that defects are detected, attributed, corrected, and trended by dealer.

A performing loan can still be a defective loan. Credit performance does not cure a disclosure error, and the absence of a member complaint does not prove the process worked.

This is as much a data-mapping problem as a disclosure problem. A system built to catch the ancillary charges it was configured to look for can still miss the ones a dealer routes through a generic field.

ECOA, Regulation B, and Fair Lending

Fair lending is easy to support as a principle and harder to demonstrate as a control. Every qualified applicant should receive consistent treatment. The governance challenge is proving that similarly situated applicants actually receive reasonably consistent decisions, pricing, stipulations, exceptions, and access to second looks, and demonstrating that with evidence rather than assurance.

Indirect lending makes this more difficult because several parties influence the result. The dealer interacts with the consumer, structures the transaction, selects which lenders receive the application, and may have discretion over pricing or compensation. The credit union makes or purchases the credit decision. A review limited to the final approval or decline can miss what happened earlier in the process.

The regulatory theory may change, but the management question does not. Can the credit union explain why similarly situated applicants received different decisions, prices, stipulations, exceptions, or access to reconsideration? Even when a statistical disparity does not by itself establish liability under a particular legal theory, an unexplained difference can identify inconsistent controls, dealer favoritism, reputation risk, or exposure under other applicable law. The practical response is to maintain a stable process that identifies and explains material differences, rather than rebuilding the monitoring program whenever Washington changes direction.

Federal enforcement has shifted since the CFPB's 2013 bulletin on indirect auto lending and dealer markup. Congress disapproved that bulletin in 2018, providing that it would have no force or effect, and the legal theory behind it, that a statistical pattern alone can establish discrimination, has continued to be argued and litigated at the state level in the years since.

More recently, federal policy has moved toward requiring evidence that a lender treated an applicant differently on purpose rather than resting on a statistical pattern alone, and other agencies may adopt a similar posture. State attorneys general and state regulators have not uniformly followed. This is an area that continues to shift, so confirm the current federal and state enforcement posture with counsel, by specific rule or guidance document, before treating any interpretation as settled.

Rather than starting with whether discrimination occurred, fair lending monitoring should begin by asking what outcomes the program is producing and whether material differences can be explained by legitimate, documented factors. A disparity is not automatically a violation. It is a reason to look closer.

What a Fair Lending Dashboard Should Track

A useful fair lending dashboard combines application, decision, pricing, exception, notice, dealer, geographic, and complaint information. Management should review trends over time and compare similarly situated applicants where the data permits. Examples include:

- Application and approval rates by dealer, geography, credit tier, and other available comparison group.
- Decline rates and principal adverse-action reasons by dealer and credit tier.
- Average APR, note rate, dealer compensation, and pricing spread by dealer and comparable credit tier.

- Pricing exceptions and waived fees by dealer, underwriter, exception type, and approving authority.
- Underwriting exception rates by dealer, underwriter, guideline, and disposition.
- Second-look request rates, approval rates after second look, and the dealers receiving the most reconsideration activity.
- Stipulation frequency, including income verification and proof-of-residence requirements, by comparable credit tier and dealer.
- Adverse-action notice timeliness, accuracy, and reason-code quality.
- Ancillary-product amount and concentration by dealer, loan amount, and comparable borrower segment.
- Complaints involving pricing, steering, discouragement, unexplained conditions, ancillary products, or discrimination allegations.
- Geographic patterns in applications, approvals, pricing, exceptions, and complaints.
- Dealer outliers requiring review, corrective action, enhanced monitoring, restriction, suspension, or removal.

The board does not need loan-level data in every meeting. It needs enough information to know whether management is testing for consistency, investigating outliers, documenting explanations, and correcting processes when differences cannot be supported.

Case Study: The Unwritten Standard

A credit union establishes a formal second-look procedure allowing dealers to request manual reconsideration of applications the automated decision engine initially referred or declined. On paper, the policy is fair, structured, and available to every approved dealership in the network.

Over time, informal relationships develop. F&I managers at three top-producing franchise dealerships obtain the direct phone numbers and personal email addresses of senior underwriters. When a deal is declined on a Saturday afternoon, these managers text the underwriter directly to argue compensating factors. The underwriters, eager to keep the relationship with high-volume stores intact, routinely issue manual overrides and waive income-documentation stipulations. Smaller and rural dealerships, meanwhile, receive a standard automated decline notice with no direct line to an underwriter, and assume the system's decision is final.

A fair lending audit finds that the three high-volume dealerships account for 62 percent of all manual underwriting overrides and stipulation waivers, despite submitting an applicant credit profile that is statistically identical to the rest of the network. There is no evidence of intentional discrimination. The credit union had nonetheless built an unwritten, multi-tiered underwriting system that provided preferential access to human review based on dealer familiarity, exactly the kind of disparate-treatment exposure ECOA and Regulation B are designed to catch.

> **Lesson:** A control is only consistent if access to it is consistent. Informal communication channels create fair lending liability regardless of whether each individual credit decision was defensible on its own.

Dealer Markup and Pricing Discretion

Dealer compensation is not inherently a fair lending problem. Unmeasured discretion is the problem. Whenever similarly situated borrowers can receive different pricing outcomes, management needs enough information to understand why.

Programs generally become more predictable when compensation is flat, capped, or tightly tiered. A flat, per-loan incentive fee limits this risk by nature, since compensation no longer varies with how an individual borrower is priced, but it does not eliminate the risk entirely: a dealer can still steer certain deals toward or away from the credit union altogether, or toward a different lender, even when every deal it does send pays the same fee. If discretion remains, the credit union should compare outcomes by dealer and comparable credit tier, investigate outliers, and document legitimate explanations.

KEY PRINCIPLE

The question is straightforward: can management explain why similarly situated borrowers received different pricing?

Case Study: The Dealer Markup Question Nobody Could Answer

To stay competitive for dealer paper, a credit union's board permits dealerships to mark up the buy rate by up to 200 basis points as compensation for placing the loan. Management monitors portfolio yield, volume, and delinquency, but not markup distribution by dealer.

During an examination, examiners compare similarly situated borrowers across identical FICO, loan-to-value, and debt-to-income tiers. One dealership consistently charges the full markup to younger, first-time, or thin-file borrowers while offering no markup to established local buyers.

When management cannot provide a documented, nondiscriminatory rationale for the different pricing, the credit union enters remediation, conducts a historical portfolio review, and replaces discretionary markup with a flat-fee compensation structure.

> **Lesson:** Unmeasured dealer discretion is a fair lending hazard. A credit union that permits discretionary rate markup has to actively monitor pricing outcomes by dealer and credit tier, so that any disparity can be explained by legitimate, documented factors rather than discovered by an examiner first.

Adverse Action Notices

Indirect lending creates predictable confusion around adverse action. The dealer and lender both participate, and each may assume the other completed the notice.

Responsibility should be assigned in writing, implemented in the workflow, and tested periodically. A delegated task is not a transferred responsibility.

Case Study: Everyone Thought Someone Else Sent It

A credit union believed its dealer platform generated adverse-action notices automatically. Several dealers believed the credit union generated them. Because no one had complained, management assumed the process was working.

During routine testing, the compliance officer selected a sample of declined applications. Several files contained no evidence that a notice had been sent. Other notices were late or used reasons that did not accurately describe the decision.

The initial reaction was to determine whether the dealer or platform had failed. The more important finding was that the process had never been thoroughly tested and verified in the first place: no one had ever reconciled declined applications against completed notices to confirm the arrangement was actually working.

> **Lesson:** A delegated task is not a transferred responsibility. If the credit union cannot verify that the notice was sent accurately and on time, it does not have an effective control.

The Military Lending Act

The Military Lending Act is frequently discussed in connection with vehicle finance because purchase-money credit secured by the vehicle may fall outside the rule's coverage. The practical risk is treating that general understanding as a substitute for transaction-specific legal analysis.

Transaction structure matters. Additional products, cash advances, refinancing, or state-specific servicemember protections may change the analysis or create separate obligations. Management should document the institution's approach, identify transactions that require escalation, and obtain current legal guidance rather than relying on an informal statement that auto loans are exempt.

This is also a technology issue. If a system cannot identify a covered borrower, an unusual transaction structure, or a state-specific restriction, the policy may exist without an executable control.

IN PRACTICE

There is a practical fix worth knowing about here. The major credit bureaus offer a covered-borrower designation as part of a standard credit pull, which flags an applicant for MLA review automatically rather than relying on staff to catch it manually. Confirm that the credit union's indirect loan credit bureau is configured to return this flag, and that the decision engine actually reads it and acts on it, rather than assuming the capability exists simply because the bureau relationship does.

State Retail Installment Sales Laws and Geographic Expansion

State retail installment sales laws may govern contract form, permitted charges, disclosures, cancellation rights, repossession practices, and other aspects of the underlying sale. State servicemember, insurance, GAP, title, lien, and consumer-protection requirements may add another layer.

A credit union operating in more than one state should treat legal inventory and change management as continuing controls. Geographic expansion is a compliance-capacity decision as much as a dealer-development one. The fact that a platform can deliver applications from another state does not mean the institution is ready to purchase them.

Case Study: The Expansion That Outran Compliance

Seeking balance sheet growth, a successful credit union expands its indirect lending footprint into an adjacent state. It connects its loan origination system to aggregator portals in the new region, and application volume begins flowing immediately. The loans fit the credit union's prime-credit underwriting standards, and early performance looks clean.

The aggregator software delivers the contracts seamlessly and the loan origination system boards them without a technical hitch, but management never conducts a pre-launch legal inventory of the neighboring state's retail installment sales act and consumer protection statutes. The new state, it turns out, requires specific statutory language on GAP cancellation refund timelines and imposes strict limits on doc-fee financing that differ from the credit union's home state.

A routine compliance review a year after launch finds that every contract purchased in the neighboring state used home-state contract forms that omitted the required statutory disclosures. The oversight creates potential consumer-remediation obligations, examination criticism, statutory exposure, and contract-enforcement questions that require state-specific legal review across the affected contracts.

> **Lesson:** Geographic expansion is compliance expansion. Software can route a loan from anywhere, but it cannot substitute for the legal inventory required to confirm an out-of-state contract complies with that state's law.

The Holder Rule in Ongoing Dealer Due Diligence

Chapter 1 introduced the Holder Rule; this section covers what it means for ongoing dealer monitoring. The FTC Holder Rule matters because a purchased consumer credit contract cannot always be separated from the underlying sale. Under the Holder Rule, a consumer may be able to assert against the credit union, as holder of the contract, claims and defenses arising from the dealer's conduct. The precise exposure depends on the claim, the contract, applicable state law, and the facts, but dealer representations, product disclosures, vehicle condition, refund administration, and complaint patterns can all become relevant even when the credit union made a sound credit decision.

That is why dealer due diligence cannot be a one-time licensing exercise. Ongoing monitoring should connect complaints, documentation defects, ancillary-product patterns, early payoffs, EPDs, chargebacks, and legal or regulatory developments. The institution is deciding whether continuing to purchase that dealer's contracts remains consistent with its own risk appetite, not managing the dealer's business.

Case Study: The Performing Dealer With the Complaint Pattern

A franchise dealership ranks as one of the credit union's top indirect partners. Delinquencies sit under 0.20 percent, charge-offs are almost nonexistent, and early payment defaults are effectively zero. On a standard scorecard, the relationship looks like a model success.

Behind that scorecard, the dealership's F&I department is packing contracts with $5,000 to $8,000 in high-margin backend products. When members realize what was added to their loans and try to cancel optional coverage inside the 30-day free-look window, the dealership delays the cancellation paperwork to keep its commission. Over twelve months, multiple members file complaints with the credit union and with state regulators over unrefunded GAP and warranty cancellations.

The credit union looks into whether the Holder Rule attaches any of that conduct to its own contracts, works with the dealer to resolve the outstanding cancellations, and, where the dealer resists, issues the refund credits itself rather than leave members waiting on a dispute between the credit union and the dealership.

> **Lesson:** Credit performance and transaction quality are not the same thing. The Holder Rule can make dealer conduct legally relevant to the contract holder, which is why a loan may perform perfectly while still carrying meaningful legal and reputation risk.

Dealer Personnel Turnover as a Risk Trigger

A dealer's transaction quality is not necessarily permanent. A change in key dealership personnel, a new general manager or F&I director, is often the trigger for a shift in either direction, and a credit union that only reviews dealer performance annually will miss it for months. Chapter 8's discussion of moving dealer risk ratings up or down covers how to act on that shift once it's detected.

Ancillary Products and Dealer Transaction Quality

Ancillary products should be evaluated as part of the credit union's full exposure to the transaction, not as separate dealer add-ons that sit outside the lending decision. Before funding, management should understand how those products affect the amount financed, borrower equity, collateral protection, cancellation and refund administration, disclosure quality, and dealer-level patterns. The key policy question is not whether the dealer may sell the products, but whether the resulting contract is one the credit union is willing to own.

Even when pricing and disclosures appear technically correct, misleading representations, obstructed cancellations, or practices that create substantial consumer harm may raise separate UDAAP concerns, distinct from whether the contract itself discloses the right numbers.

Case Study: The Fee Catch-All

A credit union's board caps aggregate ancillary products, service contracts, GAP, appearance protection, prep fees, at 15 percent of the vehicle's book value. To enforce the cap, the credit union configures its loan origination system to parse the ancillary fields coming from the dealer submission platform. The primary fields, GAP insurance and extended service contract, map cleanly and trigger the automated loan-to-value and backend-cap calculations.

A high-volume franchise dealership begins using generic secondary fields on the aggregator platform, labeled things like additional fees, protection package, or miscellaneous options, to bundle dealer-installed coatings, window tinting, and administrative prep fees totaling $1,200 to $2,500 per deal. Because the system integration was only configured to sum the primary ancillary fields, these line items flow into the amount-financed total without ever triggering the automated backend cap calculation or the Regulation Z tolerance check.

The credit union funds hundreds of contracts where total ancillary charges exceed the board's 15 percent cap. A manual file sample during an internal compliance audit finds that 14 percent of funded contracts from two specific stores violated board policy. The underlying credit scores were strong and the loans were performing, but the credit union was left holding collateral positions that were more leveraged, and less monitored, than the board had approved.

> **Lesson:** Credit quality does not guarantee contract quality. Aggregator-to-LOS data mapping has to be tested field by field, with particular attention to generic catch-all fields where dealers bundle secondary add-ons outside the automated system's rules.

Other Regulatory Areas That Still Apply

This chapter concentrates on the compliance areas most directly tied to the indirect lending decision itself: Regulation Z, ECOA and Regulation B, the Military Lending Act, state retail installment sales law, and the Holder Rule. Several other bodies of law and regulation apply to an indirect lending program without being unique to it, and they are covered here in general terms, because a program built around dealer and aggregator relationships makes it easy to assume someone else already owns them.

Who Owns Lien Perfection Obligations

When a credit union purchases a dealer-originated contract, it is relying on the dealer, the state DMV, or a title-service vendor to get its lien properly and promptly recorded. State requirements and timeframes vary, and a gap between funding and perfected lien position is a real, if usually short-lived, exposure. Dealers also routinely reassign a loan to a different funding source between origination and closing, sometimes more than once, and title or other closing documents can still reference the wrong lienholder or lender as a result. A close review of every document naming the lienholder, not just the contract itself, is a step that cannot be skipped. An aging report for unperfected titles, reviewed on a regular schedule, is the standard control. The specifics belong to your title vendor and your state's UCC and title statutes, not to this book.

BSA and AML

An indirect loan is still a transaction the credit union must independently identify and verify, not one it can treat as pre-cleared because a dealer originated it. Large cash down payments, unusual payment patterns, and identity information that arrives secondhand through a dealer all deserve the same CIP and CDD discipline as a direct loan, and the credit union's BSA officer should be looking at indirect-originated transactions specifically, not assuming the general program covers them.

GLBA and Information Security

An indirect program means sharing member data with dealers and with at least one aggregator or platform vendor, in both directions. That data-sharing relationship is a Safeguards Rule matter in its own right: what is shared, how it is secured in transit, what the vendor's own security posture looks like, and what happens if either side has an incident. This is a distinct question from the platform selection and vendor management discussion in Chapter 4, which focuses on operational fit and integration, not data security.

Business Continuity and Platform Dependency

Chapter 4 already addresses vendor management and the operational risk of relying on an aggregator or LOS platform. The same dependency is also a business continuity question. If that platform goes down for an extended period, the credit union's ability to receive, decision, and fund dealer-originated loans goes down with it, and that scenario belongs in the credit union's business continuity plan, not only in a vendor contract.

None of this changes the strategic decision this book is built around. A credit union does not need to resolve title perfection, BSA monitoring, data-sharing agreements, or business continuity planning before deciding whether prime and super-prime indirect lending through franchise dealers fits its strategy. It does need to make sure these areas get looked at by the people who actually own them, the BSA officer, the information security officer, and legal counsel, as part of the same compliance and legal review this chapter describes, rather than assuming a program review that covers fair lending and disclosure accuracy has covered everything.

Documentation Expectations

An examiner, auditor, new executive, or board member cannot evaluate what management remembers. They can evaluate what the institution documented.

Significant decisions should leave an understandable record: dealer approval, exception authority, second-look decisions, fair lending reviews, complaint investigations, corrective actions, chargebacks, restriction, suspension, removal, and decisions not to pursue available remedies.

Documentation is the evidence that judgment operated within a governed process, not paperwork added afterward.

The practical test is whether someone unfamiliar with the file can understand the issue, the facts considered, the authority used, the decision made, and the follow-up required several years later.

IN PRACTICE

In practice, this starts with the notes feature inside the loan origination or indirect origination system, used consistently to document key decisions, exceptions, and adjustments as they happen. Credit unions should also ask dealers to submit requests in writing through the indirect system itself. That is difficult to enforce fully, since a phone call or a text message is often faster, but loan officers can still be trained to summarize any phone, email, or text request from a dealer in the system notes along with the response given, so the record exists even when the original request did not come through the expected channel.

Complaint Management Is a Compliance Tool

Complaints are data. They should be classified, attributed to dealers where appropriate, reviewed for recurring themes, and incorporated into dealer scorecards. Pricing complaints, ancillary-product complaints, allegations of discouragement, unexplained stipulations, title problems, refund delays, and discrimination allegations may reveal patterns before losses appear. A dealer who generates only a handful of complaints in a year, each closed as a routine service issue, can still be showing a control weakness that only becomes visible once those complaints are grouped together rather than handled one at a time.

Preparing for an Examination Before the Examination Occurs

The best examination preparation is the reporting package management already uses. The credit union should be able to explain its program objectives, dealer approval criteria, compensation structure, adverse-action process, fair lending monitoring, complaint trends, transaction-quality standards, exception reporting, and corrective actions without creating a new set of reports after the examination notice arrives.

Examiners do not expect every institution to operate like a national lender. They do expect the institution's controls to match the size, complexity, geography, and risk of its own program. A narrow program with disciplined monitoring can be easier to defend than a rapidly growing program supported by reports that only measure volume and delinquency.

At a minimum, examiners will look for indirect-lending-specific monitoring reports covering production, delinquency, and losses by dealer, product type, and credit grade. They will also expect the credit union to produce static pool reports showing how a given vintage of loans performs over time, comparing the loss curve of one year's originations against the next. That comparison is a lagging indicator, since it can take a year or more to show up, but it is one of the clearest ways to see whether a change in underwriting improved or degraded loan performance.

Things That Get Credit Unions Into Trouble

Most compliance failures in indirect lending trace back to the same handful of assumptions:

- Assuming compliance is a department rather than a management responsibility.
- Waiting until launch to determine which laws, contracts, disclosures, and state requirements apply.
- Assuming a dealer, platform, vendor, or another department completed a required task without testing it.
- Monitoring credit performance while ignoring transaction quality and member complaints.
- Reviewing fair lending only when an examiner or auditor requests it.
- Allowing trusted dealer relationships to receive different exception or second-look treatment.
- Permitting pricing discretion without measuring outcomes by dealer and comparable credit tier.
- Expanding geographically faster than legal and compliance resources can support.

- Treating dealer due diligence as a one-time approval rather than an ongoing relationship review.
- Maintaining chargeback, recourse, or corrective-action provisions that management is unwilling to enforce.
- Confusing a legally permissible transaction with one the credit union should be willing to finance.
- Waiting for losses to validate warning signs already visible in complaints, exceptions, documentation defects, or pricing patterns.

The warning signs are usually present before the examination finding, lawsuit, or public complaint. Often management had the information; the governance failure is that the institution never connected the information into a usable view of dealer and program risk.

Chapter Summary

- Compliance is a governance responsibility. Legal interpretation may be delegated to specialists, but accountability for program design remains with management and the board.
- Every transaction should pass three tests: legal permissibility, compliance with institutional standards, and acceptable transaction quality.
- A performing loan can still contain a disclosure, documentation, fair lending, or member-treatment failure.
- Fair lending monitoring should compare decisions, pricing, stipulations, exceptions,

second looks, notices, geography, and complaints, then investigate material differences, regardless of where federal enforcement currently sits.

- Dealer compensation is not inherently the problem. Unmeasured discretion and unexplained outcomes are the problem.
- A delegated compliance task is not a transferred responsibility. Adverse-action and other shared processes must be assigned and tested.
- Geographic expansion is also compliance expansion. The approved dealer network should not grow faster than the institution's ability to understand and monitor applicable state law.
- The Holder Rule and the broader transaction make dealer conduct, ancillary products, complaints, documentation, and member treatment relevant even when credit performance is strong.
- Title and lien perfection, BSA and AML, GLBA data sharing, and business continuity all apply to an indirect program and deserve specialist review, even though none of them change the underlying strategic decision.
- The strongest compliance programs identify patterns before examiners, attorneys, or members identify them first.

Board Discussion Questions

1. How does management demonstrate that similarly situated applicants receive reasonably

consistent decisions, pricing, stipulations, exceptions, and access to second looks?

2. Which fair lending and dealer-level compliance metrics should the board receive, and what thresholds require explanation or action?
3. How are complaints, documentation defects, ancillary-product patterns, and fair lending outliers incorporated into dealer monitoring?
4. What compliance behavior would cause us to restrict, suspend, or remove a profitable dealer from the network?
5. How do we confirm that adverse-action, disclosure, and contract-review responsibilities are actually being completed?
6. What legal and compliance work must be completed before the approved dealer network expands into another state?
7. If an examiner reviewed the program tomorrow, what existing evidence would demonstrate that the board and management recognize and act on emerging risk?

CEO Action Items

1. Assign ownership for each material compliance obligation and document where responsibility is shared with a dealer, vendor, or platform.
2. Build a fair lending dashboard that includes decisions, pricing, exceptions, second looks, stipulations, adverse action, geography, and complaints.

3. Establish pre-funding and post-funding contract-quality testing, with dealer-level trending and escalation.
4. Confirm the adverse-action process through periodic file testing rather than relying on workflow assumptions.
5. Create a state-law inventory and require compliance approval before geographic expansion.
6. Incorporate complaints, ancillary-product concentration, documentation quality, and corrective actions into dealer scorecards.
7. Define the circumstances requiring enhanced monitoring, chargeback, restriction, suspension, or removal.
8. Ensure board and examiner reporting exists before volume makes the program difficult to reconstruct.
9. Confirm with the BSA officer, information security officer, and legal counsel that title and lien perfection, BSA/AML, GLBA data sharing, and business continuity planning have each been reviewed for the indirect program specifically, not assumed to be covered by existing general policies.

Chapter 6: Staffing and Dealer Relationship Management

Programs Run Through People

By the time a credit union reaches this chapter, it has decided whether indirect lending fits its strategy, tested the market opportunity, established board-approved boundaries, selected supporting technology, and identified the compliance controls intended to keep the program within acceptable risk. None of those decisions execute themselves.

People determine whether the program the board approved is the program the credit union actually operates.

Every approval, exception, stipulation, dealer conversation, complaint response, funding decision, and policy interpretation eventually passes through a person. A sound program can still drift when employees begin making small accommodations, when a dealer relationship manager becomes an unofficial underwriter, when a consultant substitutes personal judgment for the credit union's guidelines, or when one overextended employee becomes the only reason the program remains responsive.

This chapter is not an organizational-chart exercise. A credit union building or maintaining the program may not have enough people to build separate departments for underwriting, funding, dealer relations, quality control, and monitoring. That makes role clarity more important, not less. The objective is to build a human-control framework that preserves judgment without allowing relationships, production pressure, or staffing limitations to redefine the program.

Dealers want decision makers. They want answers. They want someone who can resolve a stalled transaction. The credit union should provide that access without turning accessibility into unlimited authority or mutual value into mutual exceptions.

The Human Side of Governance

Most troubled indirect programs do not fail because management announces that discipline no longer matters. They fail because responsibility becomes blurred. The underwriter assumes the dealer relationship manager has already vetted the transaction. The dealer relationship manager assumes the underwriter understands how important the relationship is. A consultant assumes management wants the same flexibility the consultant used at another lender. Senior management assumes everyone understands where the lines are.

> KEY PRINCIPLE
> **Each assumption appears reasonable. Together, they produce decisions nobody clearly owns.**

Headcount is part of the staffing question, but the central issue is whether every person influencing the program understands the difference between providing information, advocating for a relationship, making a credit decision, approving an exception, and changing the standards themselves.

Who Actually Owns the Decision?

Indirect lending creates more participants than many other consumer-lending channels. Dealers, underwriters, funding staff, dealer relationship managers, consultants, vendors, managers, executives, and automated decision systems may all influence the outcome. Influence and authority are not the same thing.

Management should be able to identify who has authority to:

- Approve loans within normal underwriting standards.
- Approve specific categories of exceptions.
- Override an automated decision or referral.
- Waive or modify stipulations.
- Grant pricing exceptions.
- Change underwriting guidelines or automated decision rules.
- Place a dealer under enhanced monitoring or probation.
- Suspend or reinstate a dealer relationship.

The answer should not depend on who happens to be available, which dealer is calling, or how important the transaction feels at the moment. Decision authority should be explicit enough that employees know when judgment is expected and when escalation is required.

Case Study: The Loan Nobody Approved

A dealer submits an application requiring several exceptions. The dealer relationship manager believes the transaction appears reasonable and forwards it to a senior underwriter with a note that the dealership has historically produced strong loans.

The underwriter reads the note as a recommendation from management. The application is approved, funded, and later becomes one of the largest losses in the program.

When management reviews the file, the dealer relationship manager explains that the note was intended only to provide relationship context. The underwriter explains that the note appeared to signal that preserving the dealer relationship justified flexibility. Neither employee believed the other had made the decision, yet both influenced it.

The credit union had an exception policy. What it lacked was a clear record identifying the decision maker, the authority used, the compensating factors accepted, and the person accountable for the exception.

> **Lesson:** When authority boundaries are unclear, influence quietly becomes decision-making.

Dealers Want Decision Makers

Dealers do not want a lender representative who can only repeat what the system already said. They want access to someone who can explain the decision, identify what information is missing, and determine whether a restructured transaction deserves another look.

Not every employee who speaks with a dealer needs exception authority, but the credit union does need a predictable escalation path. A dealer should know how to request reconsideration, what information is required, when a decision can be expected, and who owns the final answer.

Figure 6-1. Dealer communication, credit authority, and escalation should remain distinct even in a small team.

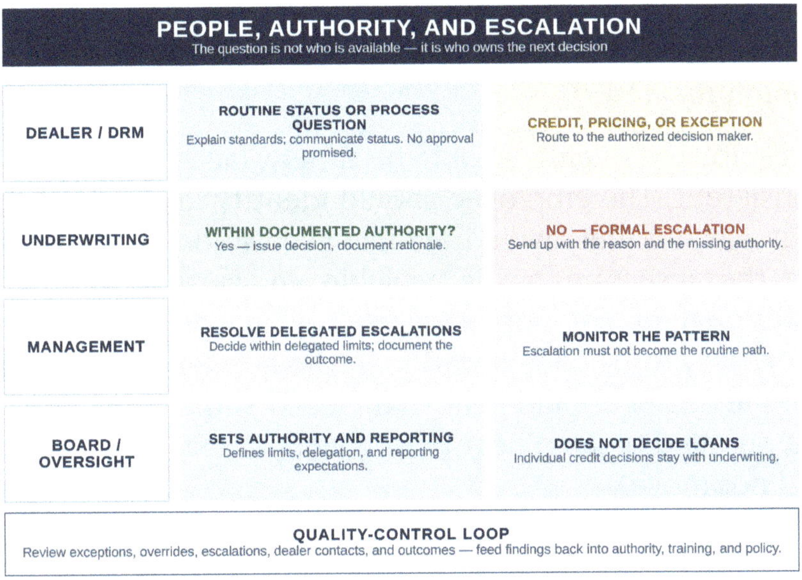

Access matters because uncertainty consumes dealer time. A clear decline is often easier to manage than an unexplained referral that sits untouched for hours. The competitive advantage comes from reaching a reliable answer while the transaction can still be completed, more than from saying yes more often.

This is also a place where even a smaller credit union can compete effectively against far larger lenders. A large bank's indirect underwriter often has no authority to explain a decision or approve same-day reconsideration. A credit union's direct access to a real decision maker can be the reason a dealer sends the next deal here instead of there.

How to Say No Without Damaging the Relationship

Every indirect program will decline transactions a dealer wants approved. The quality of the relationship often depends less on the decision than on how the decision is communicated.

A disciplined decline should be timely, fact-based, and consistent. The employee should identify the requirement that was not met, avoid personal accusations, explain whether a second look is available, and state what additional information or restructuring would be necessary for reconsideration. If the answer will remain no, the dealer should hear that clearly rather than being encouraged to keep negotiating against a standard that will not move.

The objective is to remove uncertainty while preserving respect, without defending the credit union or arguing the decision.

A decision should also never surprise the dealer after the fact. Discovering during a funding audit that an unauthorized exception was made, or adding a significant stipulation well after the member has already driven away in the vehicle, damages a dealer relationship faster than any clean decline ever could.

Case Study: The Decline That Saved the Relationship

A dealer submits a transaction materially above the credit union's maximum advance. The F&I manager calls repeatedly, arguing that the borrower has excellent credit and that another lender will approve the deal if the credit union will not.

A loan officer initially responds with vague language: the file is still being reviewed, management may consider an exception, and the dealer should wait. Two hours pass before a manager confirms that the transaction will not be approved as structured.

After reviewing the complaint, management changes the communication standard. The next similar application receives an immediate response: the requested advance exceeds the program limit, the file may be reconsidered at a specified advance with additional cash down, otherwise the dealer should place the transaction elsewhere.

The dealer does not like the answer, but it can act on it. Over time the dealership continues sending loans because the credit union becomes known for reaching a clear decision rather than keeping transactions alive with false hope.

> **Lesson:** A prompt, usable no protects the relationship better than an uncertain maybe.

The Dealer Relationship Manager Boundary

The dealer relationship manager occupies one of the most valuable and one of the most dangerous positions in the program. A strong DRM can improve communication, reduce documentation problems, identify emerging dealer concerns, and build relationships that produce consistent, higher-quality business.

The risk is advocacy. Dealer relationship managers spend their time understanding dealer needs. Underwriters spend their time evaluating risk. Those responsibilities support each other, but they are not interchangeable.

A DRM should be able to explain the program, describe documentation expectations, route a second-look request, communicate decisions, and bring dealer context to management. A DRM should not promise an approval, negotiate an exception, pressure an underwriter, or coach a dealer around automated controls.

In many resource-constrained programs, the same person serves as both dealer relationship manager and underwriter, since volume does not justify two positions. That overlap makes quality control and post-funding audits more important, not less. An independent review protects the credit union and protects the employee, who can build the dealer relationship the job requires while knowing someone else is confirming that relationship isn't becoming the underwriting standard.

Dealer Coaching and Decision-Engine Transparency

Dealers need enough information to submit accurate applications and structure transactions that fit the program. They do not need a map of every automated threshold, tolerance, and override path.

Too little information creates unnecessary referrals and frustration. Too much information invites strategic data entry and control avoidance. Management should decide what employees may explain, what belongs only in internal training, and how recurring dealer questions will be answered consistently.

The safest boundary is to explain the credit union's standards and the reason a transaction failed them without disclosing the precise mechanics necessary to manipulate an approval. When corrected documentation changes the facts, the credit union should reconsider the file. When only the presentation changes, the underlying risk has not changed.

Case Study: The Dealer Who Learned the System

A franchise dealership produces reliable volume and clean documentation. Its F&I director develops a strong working relationship with the credit union's dealer relationship manager and begins calling before difficult applications are submitted, asking whether a structure would work, which stipulation is likely required, and what usually causes a file like this to refer. The questions sound reasonable, and the DRM, wanting to save the dealer time, explains the thresholds in increasing detail over several months.

Underwriters eventually notice that applications from the dealership repeatedly land just inside the credit union's limits for loan-to-value, income variance, vehicle age, and ancillary products. A quality-control review comparing application data against funding documents finds the pattern is not coincidence. The report shows an unnatural cluster of files where stated income sits at exactly the level needed to keep the debt-to-income ratio just under the maximum allowed, a pattern real income data rarely produces on its own. Housing expense categories are selected in ways that minimize calculated obligations, and ancillary products appear in fields that do not feed every automated control.

Interviews confirm that no one taught the dealer to falsify information, and the DRM never approved a loan or intended to weaken a control. The dealership had simply learned, one well-intentioned answer at a time, how to present transactions to the system rather than how to satisfy the credit union's underlying standards. Management standardizes dealer communications, limits disclosure of internal rule mechanics, and places the dealer under manual review until data quality improves.

> **Lesson:** Explaining a standard is different from teaching a dealer how to navigate around it. Even answers meant only to help can add up to a blueprint of the decision engine.

Detecting Duplicate and Near-Duplicate Applications

One recurring dealer tactic deserves explicit attention. A deal submitted with two co-borrowers, one of whom has weak credit, gets declined. The dealer resubmits minutes later with only the stronger applicant, hoping the automated engine clears it without a human ever connecting the two files. A duplicate or near-duplicate application should be flagged automatically and reviewed by a person, not treated as a fresh submission.

Consultants, Vendors, and Third-Party Underwriting

Credit unions may use third-party underwriters or consultants to extend evening and weekend coverage, supplement experience, configure decision rules, or support launch. That can be a practical way to close a capacity gap.

The boundary is the same one Chapter 4 establishes for outsourced underwriting: a third party should apply the credit union's guidelines, not make exceptions to them. Any exception authority a consultant or vendor is given should be explicit, narrow, and reviewed the same way an employee's would be. Anything broader amounts to a second, unwritten risk appetite operating alongside the board's own.

IN PRACTICE

For example, a consultant might be authorized to approve a debt-to-income ratio up to two percentage points above the standard ceiling, and only when the file also shows a larger-than-typical down payment or substantial available revolving credit capacity as an offsetting factor. That is narrow enough to test, audit, and revoke. An unwritten, case-by-case sense of what feels reasonable is not.

Management should review decisions, exception activity, consistency, turnaround time, and subsequent performance. The third party needs feedback when its decisions begin to drift, just as an internal employee would.

KEY PRINCIPLE

Outsourcing the work does not outsource the risk.

Case Study: The Consultant Who Became the Policy

A credit union hires an experienced indirect-lending consultant to provide underwriting support during evenings and weekends. The consultant has worked for several larger lenders and knows the dealer market well.

At launch, internal managers review nearly every consultant decision. As confidence grows and volume increases, the reviews become less frequent. The consultant begins approving transactions based on compensating factors accepted by prior employers but not clearly permitted by the credit union's own guidelines.

When early delinquency begins to rise, management separates the portfolio by decision source. Consultant-approved loans show a materially higher exception rate, but many of those exceptions were never coded because the consultant viewed them as ordinary judgment.

No single decision appears reckless. The accumulated decisions reveal that the portfolio has been operating under two risk appetites: the board's written one and the consultant's experienced one.

> **Lesson:** Experience does not eliminate the need for boundaries. Unreviewed outside judgment becomes an unofficial policy.

Direct Lending Experience Is Not Indirect Lending Experience

A successful branch lender, mortgage lender, or direct consumer lender may become an excellent indirect underwriter. Management should not assume the transition is automatic. The failure mode is rarely a skills gap. It is a pacing mismatch: direct lenders are used to the rhythm of a relationship, a conversation, a follow-up call, time to think, while indirect lending runs at transactional speed and asks the underwriter to trust third-party data over a borrower interview that will never happen. Volume also arrives in bursts, and dealer pressure is immediate. The underwriter must be comfortable making a clear decision without letting speed substitute for analysis.

The skill is recognizing which applications fit automated standards, which require context, which contain unreliable data, and which dealer patterns matter beyond the individual file.

Training and Progressive Authority

New employees have not lived through the mistakes that shaped the policy. Giving them the guidelines without the history teaches the rule but not the reason.

Training should include actual applications, prior exceptions, funding defects, dealer complaints, data discrepancies, early payment defaults, and examples where a technically approvable loan still presented unacceptable transaction quality. Employees need to understand the program, not merely the decision matrix.

Authority should expand as proficiency is demonstrated. A new underwriter may begin with loans that fit automated standards, move to referred applications under review, and receive limited exception authority only after management confirms consistent judgment and documentation. The objective is to prevent confidence from growing faster than competence.

Case Study: The New Underwriter's Perfect Numbers

A newly hired underwriter quickly becomes one of the department's most productive employees. Files move quickly, documentation is complete, and nearly every decision fits the written guidelines.

Six months later, management reviews dealer-level activity and finds that the underwriter has approved a disproportionate number of transactions from two aggressive dealerships. The individual loans qualify, but the stores also generate elevated complaints, ancillary-product concentrations, and documentation corrections after approval.

The underwriter had been trained thoroughly on borrower and collateral standards. No one had taught the employee to consider dealer-level risk or to recognize when a series of technically acceptable files created a broader pattern.

Management revises training so every underwriter receives dealer scorecard information and understands which relationships require enhanced scrutiny.

> **Lesson:** A technically correct loan-level decision can still miss dealer-level risk. Employees need program context, not just underwriting rules.

Coverage, Responsiveness, and Capacity

Dealers sell vehicles when consumers are available. Evenings, weekends, holidays, vacations, and staffing absences expose the difference between a service promise and an operating model.

Chapter 4 addressed the technology needed to identify and route applications outside normal business hours. This chapter addresses the people required to resolve them. Continuous staffing is not always necessary, but the credit union does need a coverage standard it can sustain and communicate predictably.

Chapter 4 also introduced the distinction between automated decision time and final decision time. That same distinction belongs in staffing coverage: an approval that still requires an unanswered stipulation is not complete from the dealer's perspective. Coverage should therefore account for referrals, second looks, stipulation questions, documentation problems, and funding escalations, not merely the arrival of new applications.

A Program That Depends on Heroics Is Not Scalable

Some programs become successful because one employee refuses to let them fail. That person answers calls during dinner, checks the queue on weekends, clears stipulations from home, and knows every important dealer personally.

The commitment is valuable. The dependency is dangerous.

Burnout, illness, vacation, promotion, or resignation will eventually reveal the true staffing model.

KEY PRINCIPLE

If normal service requires extraordinary personal effort, the credit union has not solved the capacity problem. It has hidden it.

Succession and Key-Person Risk

Beyond real-time coverage, many programs also have an unofficial indirect person, someone who carries the platform quirks, exception history, and dealer-specific judgment that were never written down. Cross-training, shared dealer ownership, system notes, documented escalation paths, and periodic rotation are the actual controls. The goal is to make sure the program stays understandable when that person leaves.

Case Study: The Employee Who Was the Program

An indirect lending manager builds a reputation for answering dealer calls at nearly any hour. High-volume dealerships bypass the shared line and call the manager directly because questions get resolved immediately. Management sees strong dealer satisfaction and assumes the coverage model is working, until the manager takes a two-week vacation and turns off the phone.

Within days, dealers complain that the credit union has become unresponsive. Staff discover that many of the calls involved routine questions dealers had never been trained to route through the regular channel, and that employees had never been given enough information or authority to answer them consistently. The credit union responds by building shared coverage, a dealer escalation line, documented call notes, and scheduled review windows. The manager remains important, but no longer functions as the only bridge between the institution and its dealers.

> **Lesson: A service model that disappears when one employee takes leave is a key-person dependency, even when dealer satisfaction looks strong right up until the vacation.**

Compensation and Performance Management

A performance system built primarily around booked volume will produce a different program from one that measures decision quality, documentation, responsiveness, exceptions, funding accuracy, and portfolio performance.

KEY PRINCIPLE

Employees respond to the measures management chooses.

Volume still matters; a program that never books loans is not succeeding. But volume should be balanced with evidence that the volume fits the strategy and remains manageable.

Compensation tied to lending is more than a supervisory preference the board can weigh against production goals. NCUA's own regulation, 12 CFR 701.21(c)(8), generally prohibits any credit union official or employee from receiving compensation connected to a loan the credit union makes. A narrow exception allows a non-senior-management employee to receive an incentive or bonus tied to loan volume, but only under a written, board-approved policy that establishes internal controls and is reviewed for compliance at least annually. Senior management employees do not get that exception at all. The only lending-related basis permitted for them is compensation tied to the credit union's overall financial performance as a whole, not to loan volume specifically. A credit union should treat any indirect-lending incentive plan as falling under this rule from the outset, not as a compensation question to sort out with counsel after the plan is already running.

NCUA proposed changes to this regulation in February 2026 intended to clarify and loosen it, with the comment period closing in April 2026. That rulemaking had not been finalized when this chapter was written, and the underlying rule could look different by the time a program is designed. Until then, the safest working assumption is the one already in place: no incentive connected to loan volume for anyone in a senior management role, and a formal, written, board-approved policy with documented annual review before extending one to anyone else.

What to Measure

Performance measures should reflect the employee's actual role and the outcomes the employee can influence. Useful measures may include:

- Application and final-decision turnaround time, including evening and weekend performance where applicable.
- Decision accuracy and rework caused by preventable errors.

- Exception volume, type, documentation quality, and subsequent performance.
- Stipulation quality and the percentage of approvals requiring avoidable follow-up.
- Funding accuracy, aged contracts, and documentation defects.
- Dealer communication standards and unresolved escalation aging.
- Complaint patterns connected to communication, decisions, or follow-through.
- Adherence to authority limits and documentation expectations.
- Dealer-level performance trends within the employee's assigned relationships.
- Cross-training, procedure maintenance, and contribution to reducing key-person dependency.

Some of these measures, including turnaround time, documentation quality, and dealer-level performance, could support a compliant incentive policy for non-senior-management staff once the board-approved framework above is in place. Others are cleaner still, because they never touch a loan at all: the number of dealer visits completed, new franchise relationships signed, cross-training milestones reached, or documented mentorship of a newer underwriter. Those are available to any employee, including senior management, without the rule's exception process ever coming into play.

Not every measure belongs in compensation. Some belong in coaching, quality control, or management reporting. The important point is that no single production metric should become the practical definition of success.

Case Study: The Bonus Program That Worked

A credit union introduces an incentive plan intended to accelerate indirect growth. Underwriters and dealer relationship staff receive bonuses based largely on funded balances and monthly production targets, and the plan works: application response improves, booked volume increases, and dealer engagement expands.

Eighteen months after launch, management notices a rise in exception frequency, dealer concentration, and approvals near maximum advance limits. Losses have not yet increased materially because the loans are still young, but the pattern is clear enough to raise concern. The incentive plan rewards booked volume, not the quality of the decision or the strength of the funded contract.

No employee violated policy. The compensation structure simply taught staff that an exception-approved loan counted toward the bonus while a disciplined decline did not. Time spent correcting dealer documentation, challenging weak structures, or identifying a file that should not be funded reduced production without improving the measured result.

> **Lesson: Incentives shape behavior before losses appear. If performance measures reward production without equal attention to exception quality, documentation defects, complaints, and dealer-level outcomes, the program can drift long before delinquency confirms the problem.**

Dealer Relationship Manager Performance

Dealer relationship managers should not be evaluated solely on application volume or funded balances. A dealer sending applications is not necessarily sending business, and a high-volume relationship may consume more underwriting and funding capacity than it creates in value.

Performance should consider the quality of the approved dealer network: look-to-book, exception rates, documentation quality, funding quality, complaints, EPDs, early payoffs, chargebacks, ancillary-product concentration, and responsiveness to corrective action. Those measures are developed in depth later in this book; what matters here is why relationship staff need to care about them now.

A DRM should be rewarded for improving a relationship, narrowing an unproductive one, or recommending termination when the dealer no longer creates mutual value. If compensation recognizes only growth, the employee is placed in conflict with the governance role the position is supposed to support.

Communication Standards and Institutional Ownership

Dealer relationships should belong to the credit union, not to individual employees. Direct cell-phone access and personal relationships may be useful, but material requests and decisions should still enter the institution's systems.

Employees should document second-look requests, promised follow-up, exception discussions, dealer complaints, and significant changes in dealer personnel or behavior. Shared notes prevent the next employee from treating an old problem as a new surprise.

Communication standards should also define when a dealer receives proactive notice: staffing constraints, system outages, changes in funding timelines, policy changes, suspended products, or temporary manual review. Predictability is built by communicating before the dealer discovers the change through a failed transaction.

Things That Get Credit Unions Into Trouble

The staffing failures behind troubled programs are almost never a single bad hire. They look like this:

- Allowing influence to become decision authority without saying so.
- Failing to define who owns exceptions, overrides, pricing decisions, and dealer suspension.
- Allowing dealer relationship managers to function as unofficial underwriters.

- Teaching dealers the mechanics of navigating around controls rather than the standards they must meet.
- Permitting consultants or third-party underwriters to apply a different risk appetite from the one the board approved.
- Assuming strong direct-lending performance automatically translates into indirect-lending proficiency.
- Giving new employees authority before they understand dealer-level and transaction-quality risk.
- Measuring first response time while ignoring final decision time, rework, and funding readiness.
- Rewarding funded volume without balancing it against exceptions, defects, complaints, dealer quality, and subsequent performance.
- Building evening and weekend responsiveness around one employee's personal availability.
- Allowing dealer relationships and program knowledge to belong to individuals rather than the institution.
- Treating personally positive dealer relationships as evidence that monitoring can be reduced.
- Confusing accessibility with unlimited flexibility and dealer satisfaction with program quality.

These failures are rarely dramatic at first. They appear as helpful phone calls, fast decisions, trusted employees, successful consultants, and strong production. The risk emerges when the institution can no longer distinguish personal judgment from approved authority or reported activity from sustainable value.

Chapter Summary

- People determine whether the program designed in Chapters 1 through 5 survives real production pressure.
- Influence and authority are different. Approval, exception, override, pricing, and dealer-management authority should be explicit and documented.
- Dealers want decision makers, but access to decision makers should operate through predictable escalation rather than informal personal channels.
- A prompt and usable decline protects a relationship better than prolonged uncertainty.
- Dealer relationship managers should explain the program and support dealers without becoming unofficial underwriters or teaching workarounds.
- Third parties may apply the credit union's guidelines within defined authority. They should not substitute their own risk appetite.
- Indirect lending requires skills and context that do not automatically transfer from direct lending.
- Training should use real applications, dealer patterns, exceptions, complaints, and funding defects, with authority expanding as proficiency is demonstrated.

- Evening and weekend coverage should be sustainable and predictable. Heroics are not capacity.
- Succession, cross-training, institutional notes, and shared dealer ownership are risk controls.
- Compensation tied to lending is restricted by NCUA regulation, not just sound practice. Senior management may not receive loan-connected incentives at all, and any incentive for other staff requires a written, board-approved policy with annual compliance review.
- In resource-constrained programs where the same person serves as both dealer relationship manager and underwriter, independent quality control and post-funding review become more important, not less.
- A duplicate or restructured application submitted after a decline should be flagged automatically and reviewed by a person, not treated as a fresh submission.
- Dealer relationships belong to the institution, and strong relationships require continuing monitoring.

Board Discussion Questions

1. Who has authority to approve exceptions, override automated decisions, grant pricing flexibility, and suspend dealer relationships, and can management demonstrate that actual practice matches that authority?

2. Does our staffing model provide sustainable evening, weekend, vacation, and absence coverage, or does it depend on individual heroics?
3. How do we prevent dealer relationship management from becoming unofficial underwriting?
4. What decisions may consultants or third-party underwriters make, and how does management verify they remain within our guidelines?
5. Does our incentive structure comply with NCUA's restrictions on loan-connected compensation, and do we have the board-approved policy and annual review the exception requires?
6. Which performance measures and compensation structures could unintentionally reward volume over quality?
7. How would the program operate if its most knowledgeable employee left tomorrow?
8. Are dealer relationships owned by the institution, with documented history and shared access, or by individual employees?
9. What evidence tells us employees understand dealer-level and transaction-quality risk, not merely loan-level underwriting rules?
10. In roles where dealer relationship management and underwriting responsibilities overlap, what independent review confirms that the relationship isn't shaping the credit decision?
11. How does our system detect and route a duplicate or restructured application submitted after a decline?

CEO Action Items

1. Document decision authority for approvals, exceptions, overrides, pricing, stipulation waivers, dealer probation, suspension, and reinstatement.
2. Separate dealer relationship responsibilities from underwriting authority and establish an escalation path dealers can use consistently.
3. Define communication boundaries so employees can explain standards without disclosing internal rule mechanics or coaching around controls.
4. Establish written authority limits and review requirements for consultants and third-party underwriters.
5. Build progressive training and authority for new indirect-lending staff using actual files, dealer patterns, and documented lessons.
6. Define sustainable evening, weekend, holiday, vacation, and outage coverage, including final-decision and funding support rather than application receipt alone.
7. Identify key-person dependencies and reduce them through cross-training, system notes, shared dealer ownership, and succession planning.
8. Review incentive and performance measures to ensure funded volume is balanced with quality, exceptions, defects, complaints, dealer performance, and compliance with authority limits.

9. Confirm that any loan-connected incentive plan has a written, board-approved policy, defined internal controls, and at least annual compliance review, consistent with NCUA's compensation restrictions, and that no senior management employee receives compensation tied to loan volume.
10. Confirm whether any dealer relationship manager also functions as an underwriter, and if so, ensure quality control and post-funding review operate independently of that person.
11. Confirm the loan origination system flags duplicate or restructured applications submitted after a decline for mandatory human review.
12. Require material dealer requests, decisions, and follow-up commitments to be documented in institutional systems.
13. Begin dealer scorecard reporting early enough that relationship staff learn to manage for mutual value before the network expands.

Chapter 7: Dealer Onboarding and Launch

Where Decisions Meet the Dealership

By this point, the credit union has decided what kind of indirect program it wants, where it can compete, what risks the board will accept, how technology will execute the underwriting standards, what compliance controls apply, and who has authority to make and escalate decisions. Chapter 7 is where those decisions meet an actual dealership.

For many credit unions, that relationship will not begin with a separately negotiated dealer agreement. It will begin through an aggregator or network such as CUDL, RouteOne, or Dealertrack. One of the reasons to use a network is that the platform has already connected with the dealer, established common operating terms, and reduced the need for every lender to repeat the same contracting process.

That convenience changes the credit union's onboarding work. It does not eliminate it. Management still has to understand what the network reviews, what the network agreement covers, what remains the credit union's responsibility, which dealers the credit union will accept, and how a dealer will be restricted or removed when the relationship no longer fits.

Throughout this chapter, the normal model is aggregator-supported onboarding. Direct dealer contracting is treated as an exception for institutions that have intentionally chosen to manage the additional legal and administrative work themselves.

The purpose of dealer onboarding is therefore to decide whether the aggregator's process, combined with the credit union's own selection and monitoring, is enough for the program the board approved.

Onboarding Is a Risk Decision

A dealer may already be part of the aggregator network before the credit union joins. Depending on the platform and configuration, a broad dealer population may be visible or available immediately. That should not be confused with a management decision to accept every dealer.

Management should separate three events: the aggregator has accepted the dealer into its network, the credit union has decided to include the dealer in its own program, and the dealer has earned broader access after an initial operating period. The platform may make the first event easy. Management owns the other two.

The practical control is an actively maintained approved-dealer list. The credit union should know which dealers are included, which are excluded, why each decision was made, and who has authority to change the list.

Figure 7-1. Dealer lifecycle from network eligibility through ongoing monitoring and removal.

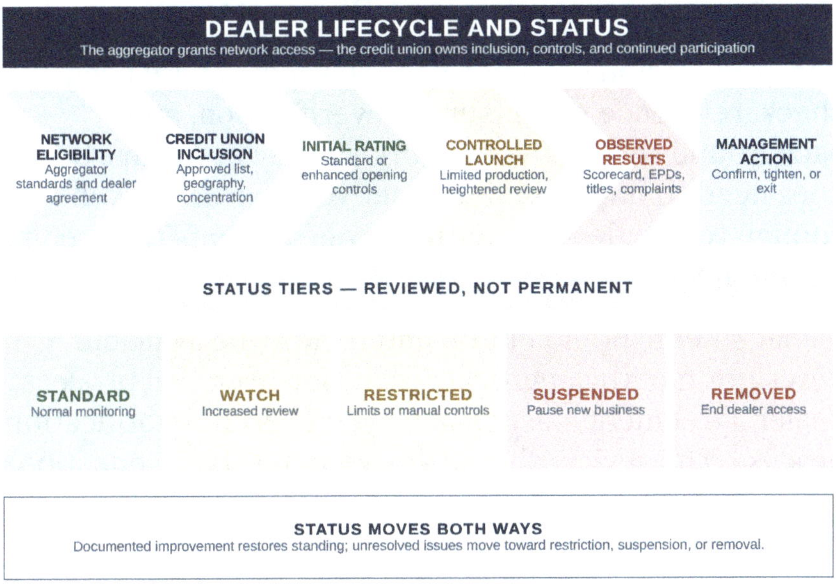

Relying on Aggregator Due Diligence

Relying on aggregator due diligence is one of the principal reasons a credit union uses an aggregator in the first place. CUDL, for example, markets the network to dealers as access to many credit unions through a single agreement. That structure reduces duplicate contracting and makes the channel practical for institutions that do not have a dealer-compliance department.

The examples in this chapter draw on CUDL specifically, since it is the network with the author's deepest direct operating experience. RouteOne and Dealertrack should raise the same questions, but their specific processes, agreements, and controls may work differently. If your credit union uses one of them, confirm the equivalent answers with that network directly rather than assuming this chapter's description of CUDL transfers over.

The credit union does not need to repeat every license check, reference call, insurance verification, and background review the network already performs, but it does need to understand the network's process well enough to decide whether the process meets the credit union's needs.

Management should obtain and review the available description of the aggregator's dealer-approval process, dealer agreement, suspension practices, and notification process. The review should answer a few basic questions:

- What minimum standards must a dealer meet to enter and remain in the network?
- How are licensing, ownership changes, complaints, fraud concerns, and other material events handled?
- What information will the aggregator provide to participating credit unions?
- Can the credit union include or exclude individual dealers and dealer groups?
- How quickly can access be restricted when the credit union identifies a problem?
- Which remedies are handled through the network agreement, and which require the credit union to act directly?

If the answers are adequate for the credit union's risk appetite, reliance is reasonable. If the process does not cover a concern the credit union considers material, management can add a targeted review, restrict the dealer, or decline to activate the relationship.

KEY PRINCIPLE

The goal is not endless due diligence. The goal is informed reliance.

Case Study: The Franchise Name That Wasn't Enough

A franchise dealership is already active in the aggregator network and has a long operating history. The credit union includes the store based on franchise standing, local reputation, and the network's existing approval.

What management does not notice is a recent ownership and leadership change. The new owner centralizes title processing at another store, replaces the F&I team, and changes the ancillary-product strategy. The name stays the same while the operating risk changes.

Title delays and member complaints begin appearing during the first several months. The aggregator's original approval was accurate when made; it described the dealer at an earlier point in time.

The credit union adds ownership and management changes to its own dealer-maintenance review rather than attempting to rebuild the aggregator's entire due-diligence process.

> **Lesson:** Aggregator approval is a starting point. Material changes still require a fresh management decision.

Assigning the Initial Dealer Risk Rating

Every dealer included in the credit union's program should receive an initial risk rating. The rating does not need to be complex. Its purpose is to determine how cautiously the relationship should begin.

This step is especially important in a new program because every dealer is new to the credit union, even if the dealer has years of experience in the aggregator network. Over time, the work becomes more focused. Dealers with a proven record move into normal annual maintenance, while new, changed, or higher-risk relationships receive more attention.

The initial rating may consider franchise status, ownership stability, location, expected volume, dealer-group concentration, experience available through the aggregator, title practices, complaint information, and any unusual product or operating concerns.

The rating should determine opening controls. A well-established local franchise dealer may begin with standard review. A newly added dealer, a store under new ownership, or a relationship outside the normal footprint may begin with lower volume limits, manual review, enhanced title tracking, or a shorter follow-up cycle.

The ongoing scorecard comes later; what gets decided here is how the relationship begins.

Concentration Is an Onboarding Gate

Chapter 3 established concentration as a board-approved boundary. Chapter 7 makes it an inclusion decision. Before adding another dealer, management should consider the volume the relationship could produce and whether the credit union has room within its dealer, dealer-group, geography, manufacturer, staffing, liquidity, and portfolio limits.

Dealer count can be misleading. Auto malls may place many franchise names on one large property while the stores are owned by one or two dealer groups. Several rooftops may share ownership, F&I management, title staff, product vendors, and technology. A disruption at the group level can therefore affect several dealer records at once.

The onboarding question goes beyond whether one more storefront is acceptable to whether the underlying economic and operational relationship fits the concentration the board intended.

> ***Case Study: The Fifth Dealer That Was Really the First Dealer***

A credit union includes five franchise dealerships and reports that no individual store is expected to exceed its opening concentration limit. Each has a different name and platform identifier.

Later, management learns that four stores share common ownership, centralized F&I leadership, one title department, and the same ancillary-product providers. The dealer report showed five relationships.

Operationally, the credit union had one dominant group and one independent store.

When the shared title department experiences turnover, missing-title volume rises across four dealer records at the same time.

Management begins tracking concentration by both rooftop and ownership group.

> **Lesson:** Count economic and operational relationships, not storefronts.

Geographic Discipline at Launch

For many programs, the safest launch boundary is the home state. Out-of-state origination adds differences in contract forms, title processes, collections law, repossession requirements, ancillary-product rules, and consumer protections. A borrower who later relocates is an ordinary servicing event. Deliberately originating in several states is a different strategy.

A platform can route an application from another state immediately. That does not mean the credit union is ready to purchase it. If management later chooses to expand, legal, compliance, servicing, title, and system readiness should be confirmed before the additional dealers are included.

The default should be simple: start where the credit union already understands the operating environment. Expand only when the expected value justifies the added legal and operational burden.

Understand the Agreement Structure

Management does not need to draft a dealer agreement, but it does need to understand the agreement structure supporting the program.

In an aggregator model, counsel should review the agreement the credit union signs with the aggregator and the standard agreement or operating terms the aggregator uses with dealers. The objective is to identify the major protections, responsibilities, remedies, and gaps that affect the credit union, rather than to negotiate every provision.

The review should stay at the concept level. Does the arrangement address accurate application and transaction information, document delivery, title work, fraud and misrepresentation, access to records, ancillary-product cancellations, chargebacks or repurchase, information security, suspension, and continuing obligations? If a concept is missing or unclear, management should ask the aggregator and counsel how the risk is handled.

Direct contracting requires substantially more work. A credit union that chooses to sign its own dealer agreements assumes responsibility for legal drafting, execution, storage, amendments, enforcement, and consistency across dealers. That path may be appropriate for a larger or highly experienced program. It is not the default model recommended for the programs this book addresses.

KEY PRINCIPLE

The credit union's job is not to negotiate every dealer relationship. The credit union's job is to understand the relationship it is relying on.

Title and Lien Controls at Onboarding

Who is expected to perform title and lien work, and how exceptions are handled, gets decided at onboarding. The chapter does not attempt to prescribe state title law or draft title provisions.

Management should understand how title responsibilities are assigned, monitored, and escalated when problems occur. The credit union still needs an aging report and someone responsible for follow-up.

For a new or higher-risk dealer, management may consider a stronger funding control, including requiring evidence that the lien has been recorded before funds are released where the process and state system make that practical. That is a significant hurdle and is not appropriate for every dealer, but it shows how the initial risk rating can change launch conditions.

The Dealer as Introducer: Identity and Fraud Information

Chapter 5 flagged identity verification as an obligation the indirect program creates without being unique to it. Onboarding is where that principle becomes a practical question. The dealer introduces the applicant and transmits identifying information. The credit union still owns its risk-based customer-identification, verification, fraud-monitoring, and reporting responsibilities.

Case Study: The Broker Who Sold Cars He Did Not Own

This case study is drawn from public federal court records rather than being a composite. A California auto broker offered customers vehicles that were not in his dealership's inventory, proposing to obtain them from other dealerships. He received up-front payments from the customers or their banks and did not pass that money to the selling dealerships, spending it on business and personal expenses instead.

To keep transactions moving, he signed the customers' names on sales documents and loan applications, causing banks to issue loans without the customers' knowledge or authorization. The conduct involved at least 48 vehicles and more than $2 million in fraudulently obtained goods and funds.

The broker was convicted of bank fraud and aggravated identity theft and sentenced to four and a half years in federal prison. The scheme affected buyers, outside dealers, and lenders at the same time. (United States v. Scott Radtke, U.S. District Court for the Eastern District of California, sentenced January 2023. Facts drawn from the Department of Justice announcement issued by the U.S. Attorney's Office for the Eastern District of California.)

Not every broker relationship will fail. But a transaction involving a vehicle outside the seller's inventory creates additional parties, additional movement of funds, and additional opportunities for documents and ownership to separate from reality.

> **Lesson:** When the seller does not control the vehicle being financed, verify the transaction before funding rather than relying on documents alone.

Confirming how identity information flows through the dealer does not require a separate dealer agreement drafted by the credit union. It requires management to confirm how identity information enters the system, what the aggregator and dealer verify, what the credit union verifies independently, and how exceptions are stopped before funding.

Unless a dealer has been formally engaged and overseen as the credit union's agent for a specific CIP function, dealer-provided information should be treated as input rather than completed verification. The operating question is straightforward: does the credit union's own process form a reasonable belief that it knows the applicant's identity before the loan is booked?

Large or unexplained cash down payments, identity mismatches, overlapping applications, altered documents, and concerns raised by the dealer should have a clear path to fraud or BSA review.

Member Information and Data Sharing

Chapter 5 also introduced GLBA data-sharing obligations in general terms. Onboarding is where the credit union confirms those obligations are actually addressed, whether through the aggregator's agreements or its own. An indirect program moves sensitive information among the dealer, aggregator, loan-origination system, and credit union, and management should understand those data flows and involve the information-security officer in the review.

For many credit unions, the practical work is reviewing the aggregator arrangement, security materials, incident-notification process, access controls, and dealer-facing requirements rather than writing a separate set of dealer data clauses.

The core questions are whether information is transmitted through approved channels, whether access is limited to authorized users, how incidents are reported, and how access is removed when a dealer or employee leaves the network. Counsel and information security can determine whether the existing agreements and controls adequately address those concepts.

Ancillary-Product Providers

The transaction-quality limits set in Chapter 3 assume the products inside a deal will be administered by somebody who is still in business. At onboarding, test that assumption, because another party's performance can affect the member and the contract long after funding.

At onboarding, management should understand which GAP, service-contract, and other material product providers commonly appear in the dealer's transactions and whether the aggregator supplies information or controls concerning those providers. A targeted review may be appropriate when an unfamiliar provider, unusual product concentration, complaint pattern, or refund problem appears.

The practical question is whether management knows who is expected to process claims, cancellations, and refunds, and what happens when that party does not perform.

This connects to the Holder Rule discussion in Chapter 5. If the provider disappears and the dealer cannot resolve the issue, the member will still look to the credit union holding the contract, and the credit union may face claims, defenses, complaint pressure, or a remediation decision depending on the facts and applicable law.

Case Study: The Refund From a Company That No Longer Existed

A dealer sells a financed service contract administered by a small outside company. The product is described as cancellable, but the credit union does not know the administrator because the dealer, not the credit union, selected the product.

A member later cancels after the administrator has ceased operations. The dealer says the administrator owes the refund. The administrator no longer responds. The member continues paying interest on an amount tied to coverage that is no longer available.

The loan continues to perform, but the dispute becomes a dealer, member, and contract-holder problem.

Management begins identifying recurring product providers and uses complaints and refund experience to decide when a dealer or product requires additional review.

> **Lesson:** A refundable product is only as reliable as the parties responsible for performing the refund.

Recourse, Repurchase, and Practical Remedies

Management should understand what remedies are available when a dealer transaction fails. In an aggregator model, those remedies may come from the network agreement rather than a contract negotiated directly by the credit union.

The concepts to confirm are straightforward: what happens when the dealer submits fraudulent information, a loan defaults immediately, title cannot be perfected, documents are defective, or an ancillary-product refund is not paid? The remedy may be correction, reimbursement, chargeback, repurchase, suspension, or termination. Counsel should advise management on the meaning and limitations of the applicable agreement language.

IN PRACTICE

The arrangement should also provide a practical recovery method. Some programs permit eligible amounts owed by the dealer to be deducted from future funding or reserves. Others rely on the aggregator to administer chargebacks or repurchase claims.

The governance question is not how the clause is drafted. It is whether the credit union has a realistic path to recover an amount the dealer owes. Management should confirm whether the aggregator's daily settlement process actually applies this kind of offset automatically, or whether the credit union has to manually initiate the clawback through the network's portal each time.

Case Study: The Repurchase Provision Nobody Intended to Use

A dealer relationship produces strong volume. Several contracts later show altered income documents and inaccurate trade information.

The aggregator agreement appears to provide a repurchase process, but no one at the credit union has used it before. Management hesitates because the dealer is important and the process is unfamiliar.

The delay shifts the cost of documented dealer conduct toward the credit union and creates uncertainty for staff. Management eventually works through the aggregator, documents the evidence, suspends new business, and invokes the available remedy.

Afterward, the credit union assigns clear authority for raising claims through the network and includes that process in dealer-management training.

> **Lesson:** Knowing a remedy exists is not the same as being prepared to enforce it.

A Controlled Launch

Aggregator representatives and dealers naturally want a new lender activated quickly. Speed is part of the platform's value. The credit union should still control the final inclusion decision.

System administrators should not activate a dealer until the credit union has completed its own review, assigned the initial risk rating, confirmed geographic and concentration limits, identified authorized contacts, and established the opening controls. Where a platform makes a broad dealer population available by default, management should actively maintain the include and exclude list rather than treating the default population as approved.

Opening controls may include a volume cap, manual review, title tracking, application-data checks, or a scheduled early review. The purpose is to test whether the dealer produces the kind of business management expected, not to create months of delay.

The initial period should end when evidence supports expansion, not merely because a calendar date arrives.

Expansion Must Be Earned

Higher volume limits, reduced review, additional locations, and broader access should follow evidence rather than dealer pressure or elapsed time.

The initial decision relies partly on the aggregator's process and the dealer's existing reputation. Expansion should rely on the credit union's own experience with documentation quality, title performance, data accuracy, member complaints, responsiveness, and early loan performance.

Ongoing scorecards and performance monitoring take over once enough history exists.

Suspension, Removal, and Related Dealers

When a dealer no longer fits the program, management should be able to stop new submissions quickly while continuing to manage loans and unresolved items already on the books.

A serious problem at one store may also raise a broader question. Fraud, compromised credentials, repeated document manipulation, or another systemic issue may involve shared ownership, personnel, systems, or processes across affiliated stores. Management should determine whether the issue is limited to one location before allowing related dealerships to continue without review.

The response may involve one store, several stores, or the entire group. The governance responsibility is to investigate the full exposure and use the suspension authority available through the platform or agreement. Management should not assume either that all related stores are defective or that the problem must be isolated.

Removal should include platform access, pending applications, unresolved titles, open refunds, complaints, recourse claims, and any other item that survives the end of new business. The aggregator may administer part of this process, but the credit union still needs one internal owner who tracks every open item to closure.

Case Study: The Dealer That Was Removed but Never Really Left

A credit union decides to stop accepting new business from a dealer after repeated documentation problems.

The dealer remains active on the platform while employees determine who can change the setting. Several pending applications remain in the queue. Missing titles, open product refunds, and a disputed chargeback are assigned to different employees.

One pending application is approved because the underwriter assumes the decision applies only to applications received after the notice.

Management creates a formal removal process with a single owner, immediate access controls, treatment of pending transactions, and a list of surviving items that remain open until resolved.

> **Lesson:** Removing a dealer is a process, not a status change.

Things That Get Credit Unions Into Trouble

Onboarding mistakes are easy to make precisely because the platform makes the first step so simple:

- Assuming aggregator approval means every network dealer fits the credit union's strategy.

- Repeating the aggregator's entire due-diligence process instead of understanding it and filling only material gaps.
- Failing to maintain an active include and exclude list.
- Using franchise names or rooftop counts without identifying common ownership and shared operations.
- Opening the program outside the home state before legal and operational capacity is ready.
- Reading the agreement as a legal document but never translating its major protections and remedies into operating responsibilities.
- Treating dealer-transmitted identity information as completed verification.
- Assuming the aggregator solves every information-security, title, refund, or complaint issue.
- Knowing chargeback or repurchase rights exist but not knowing how to invoke them through the network.
- Allowing platform urgency to activate a dealer before credit union approval is complete.
- Removing one store without considering whether the same issue may exist at affiliated locations.
- Turning off new business without assigning ownership of pending applications, titles, refunds, and open claims.

The recurring mistake is confusing network convenience with transferred accountability. Aggregators reduce contracting and administrative friction. The credit union still owns its dealer selection, lending decisions, portfolio, and member experience.

Chapter Summary

- For many credit unions, dealer onboarding will occur through an aggregator rather than through separately negotiated dealer agreements.
- Relying on aggregator due diligence is reasonable when management understands the process and decides it meets the credit union's needs.
- The credit union should actively maintain its own approved-dealer list even when the platform makes a broad network available.
- Every included dealer should receive an initial risk rating that determines opening controls. Chapter 8 owns ongoing performance scoring.
- Concentration should be measured by ownership group and shared operations, not only by rooftop.
- The home state is the most practical launch boundary for many programs. Out-of-state origination should be a deliberate expansion decision.
- Management should understand the credit union and dealer agreements used by the aggregator. Counsel should interpret the language and identify material gaps.
- Title, identity, data-sharing, ancillary-product, and remedy controls should focus on who owns

the task and how the credit union confirms it worked.

- Recourse, chargeback, and repurchase provisions matter only when management understands how to use them through the network.
- Technical activation should follow the credit union's inclusion decision and opening controls.
- A problem at one location may require review of affiliated stores that share ownership, personnel, systems, or processes.
- Removal ends new business, but pending transactions, titles, refunds, complaints, and claims still require an accountable owner.

Board Discussion Questions

1. What dealer due diligence does the aggregator perform, and what material risks remain for the credit union to review?
2. Who owns the credit union's dealer include and exclude list, and how often is it reviewed?
3. What initial risk ratings and opening controls will management use?
4. How does management identify common ownership and dealer-group concentration?
5. Is the program limited to the home state, and what approval would be required to expand?
6. Has counsel reviewed both the credit union's aggregator agreement and the dealer-facing terms relevant to our risk?

7. How do management and staff invoke chargeback, repurchase, suspension, or other remedies through the network?
8. What must a dealer demonstrate before opening controls are relaxed?
9. When a serious issue appears at one store, who evaluates affiliated dealerships?
10. If a dealer were removed tomorrow, who would own pending applications, titles, refunds, complaints, and open claims?

CEO Action Items

1. Obtain and review the aggregator's dealer-approval process, dealer-facing agreement or operating terms, and suspension process.
2. Document which parts of dealer due diligence the credit union relies on the aggregator to perform and which targeted checks remain internal.
3. Establish and maintain an approved-dealer include and exclude list with clear change authority and decision history.
4. Assign an initial dealer risk rating and opening controls before activation.
5. Map common ownership and shared F&I, title, product, and management functions before measuring concentration.
6. Limit launch to the home state unless legal, compliance, servicing, title, and system readiness support expansion.

7. Have counsel review the agreement structure and explain the major responsibilities, remedies, and gaps to management in operational terms.
8. Coordinate identity and data transmission with the BSA and information-security officers without duplicating the aggregator's process unnecessarily.
9. Document how title escalation, refund disputes, chargebacks, repurchase requests, suspension, and removal are handled through the network.
10. Restrict activation permissions and require a completed internal approval before a dealer is included.
11. Create a dealer-removal checklist with one accountable owner for all surviving items.

Chapter 8: Dealer Performance Monitoring

Relationships Change After Approval

By the end of Chapter 7, the dealer has been approved, assigned an initial risk rating, activated through the aggregator, and allowed to begin producing loans. Dealer risk management is only getting started.

Most indirect lending problems do not arise because management approved an obviously unacceptable dealer. They arise because a dealer relationship changed after approval and the credit union did not recognize the change soon enough. Ownership changes. F&I employees turn over. Title operations weaken. Complaints increase. Application quality changes. A relationship that once fit the program may no longer fit it.

The reverse can also occur. A dealer that begins under enhanced review may demonstrate clean documentation, strong title performance, acceptable credit quality, and reliable responsiveness. That relationship may earn broader access and lower oversight.

Chapter 7 established how a dealer relationship begins. Chapter 8 establishes how management decides whether the relationship should expand, remain unchanged, be corrected, be restricted, or end.

Monitoring exists to support decisions while management still has time to change the outcome.

Monitoring After Launch

Every approved dealer should be monitored against a consistent set of core measures. The discipline matters more than the exact number of measures, and a small program is better served by a handful of measures reviewed reliably than a long list reviewed occasionally.

A useful monitoring process answers three questions: is the relationship getting better, staying the same, or getting worse? What evidence supports that conclusion? What management response follows from it?

Review frequency should match how quickly a measure can change and how much damage a delay could cause, not a single calendar rule applied to everything. A workable schedule for a disciplined program looks like this. For a new dealer, review performance monthly for the first three months. Patterns do not usually shift week to week, but an early problem is worth catching quickly, and volume is still low enough that a monthly look is not a burden. After that initial period, and for every established dealer going forward, review all eight core measures quarterly. A single cadence is easier for a small program to actually sustain than a mix of quarterly and annual review dates spread across different measures, and every one of the eight core measures changes quickly enough to be worth a quarterly look.

A quarterly review that actually happens every quarter is worth more than a monthly review that stops happening after the second month. Set a schedule management can sustain, not the most frequent schedule that sounds thorough on paper.

Dealer management, underwriting, funding, collections, compliance, and executive management may each see a different part of the relationship. A complete view usually requires more than one department.

KEY PRINCIPLE

The purpose of dealer monitoring is not to describe the past. It is to give management time to change the future.

The Dealer Scorecard

The dealer scorecard promised earlier and the initial dealer risk rating assigned at onboarding now turn into an ongoing management process.

A dealer scorecard is intended to show whether the dealer is producing the kind of business the credit union expected, operating within standards, treating members acceptably, and responding when problems occur, not to identify the most popular dealer or reward the largest relationship.

For many credit unions, eight measures are enough to govern an indirect program well, provided they are the right eight. Together they answer four questions: is the dealer sending good paper and are those loans staying on the books as expected, is the dealer's back office functioning, does the dealer's volume fit the program, and is the dealer creating complaint, reputational, or regulatory exposure. Adding more measures does not answer those questions any better. It mostly makes the scorecard harder to keep current, which is exactly the kind of complexity that causes monitoring to stop happening.

The companion Dealer Scorecard Tool supplies the calculations, weighting, and rating framework built around these eight measures. Each measure converts to a simple 1, 2, or 3 risk score, low, medium, or high, and the four category averages combine into a single composite risk index from 1.00 to 3.00. This chapter explains what the eight measures are and why each one earns its place. Appendix A provides the structural blueprint.

Figure 8-1. Weighted scorecard results inform, but do not replace, management action.

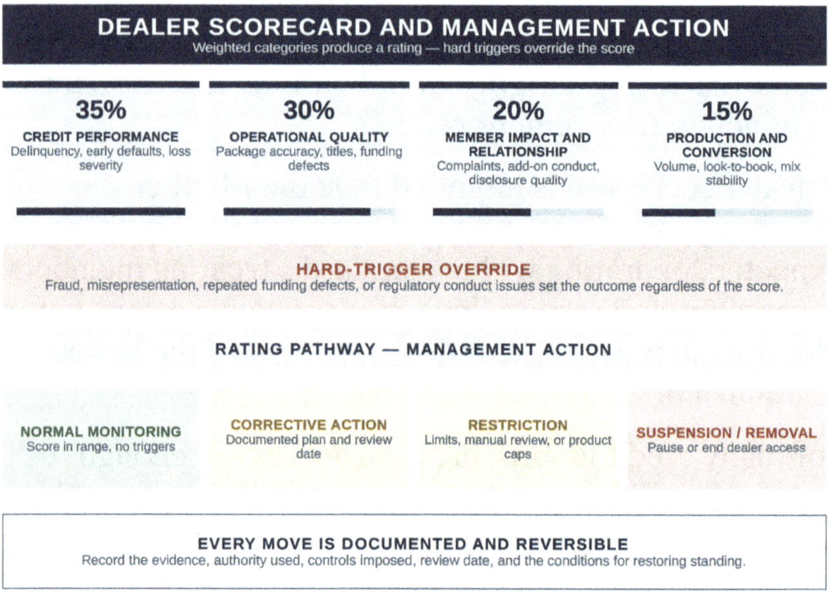

In the companion tool, credit performance and operational quality together carry roughly two-thirds of the composite weight, while production and conversion carries the smallest share. Whatever weighting a credit union ultimately calibrates, operational quality and credit performance should outweigh raw production. A high-volume dealer should never be able to mathematically offset high exception rates, repeated defects, weak payment performance, or member harm simply by sending more applications and loans.

Credit Performance: Is the Dealer Sending Good Paper?

- Delinquency, tracked at 60 days past due and beyond.
- Early payment defaults.
- Early payoffs, since a loan that pays off well before expected can mean the loans are not staying on the books long enough to generate the return the credit union priced for.

Operational Quality: Is the Dealer's Back Office Functioning?

- Titles open beyond 60 days after funding.
- Loan package quality, meaning the rate of major defects that require a contract to be re-signed, an approved amount exceeded, an incorrect rate or term, or a major structural error, not the routine missing initial or minor correction that shows up on nearly every funding package.

Production and Conversion: Does the Dealer's Volume Fit the Program?

- Volume, meaning application and funded volume relative to what the credit union expected from the relationship.
- Look-to-book ratio.

Member Impact and Relationship: Is the Dealer Creating Reputational or Regulatory Risk?

- Member complaints attributed to the dealer or the transaction.

These eight measures, combined with the hard escalation triggers described below, are enough to run a defensible, sustainable monitoring program. A credit union with more capacity and a longer operating history may eventually add measures. It should not start there.

Early payment defaults, title aging, and member complaints are tracked as counts rather than rates. A dealer sending ten loans a quarter and a dealer sending two hundred should not be held to a raw count that only makes sense at one of those two scales forever, but early in a program, or for a lower-volume dealer, a small raw count is a more stable signal than a rate with too small a denominator to mean anything. As dealer volume grows, the credit union should revisit whether a given measure is better tracked as a rate.

Responsiveness and cooperation still matter, and they are not on this list. A dealer's willingness to communicate a problem, meet a deadline, and cooperate with a review is exactly the kind of judgment a scorecard cannot reduce to a number. It belongs in the corrective action and rating discussions later in this chapter as something management weighs directly, not as a ninth measure competing for a place on the scorecard.

The scorecard should ultimately force a question numbers alone cannot answer: would management approve this dealer again today? That judgment should be anchored in observable facts, including how many unresolved issues remain open, whether corrective actions hold, and how much extraordinary staff attention the relationship consumes. The answer should not substitute for data, but it should not be avoided merely because it requires judgment.

A Score Is Not a Decision

A composite score can simplify reporting, but a mathematically acceptable total should not erase a serious control failure. A scorecard organizes judgment. It does not replace it. Strong volume and low delinquency should not offset documented fraud, repeated title defects, unresolved member refunds, or failure to cooperate with an investigation.

Scorecards work best when they combine weighted measures with hard escalation triggers. Some risks are too important to average out, and a hard escalation trigger should supersede the weighted score entirely rather than simply pulling it down. In the companion tool, three triggers override the composite risk index outright and return a suggested rating of immediate review, regardless of how favorable the underlying numbers look: confirmed fraud, a compliance or legal failure, and a failure to cure. Appendix A defines each one.

Immediate review is a scorecard output, not a final decision. It tells management to look now rather than wait for the next quarterly cycle. What happens next, correction, restriction, suspension, or removal, is still the judgment call described later in this chapter and in Chapter 7.

Early Payment Defaults: The Earliest Warning Signal

Few dealer metrics provide an earlier warning than an early payment default. A loan that fails almost immediately may reflect borrower hardship, but repeated EPDs from one dealer can also indicate fraud, inflated income, weak verification, payment manipulation, aggressive sales practices, or poor transaction quality.

Management should review EPDs by dealer, F&I employee where available, underwriter, credit tier, funding date, and cause rather than treating them only as collection events.

An EPD review should ask whether the borrower ever made a payment, whether contact information was accurate, whether income and identity data were reliable, whether the vehicle and trade matched the approved transaction, and whether similar facts appear in other loans from the same dealer.

Not every first-payment problem begins with weak credit or fraud. In an indirect transaction, the borrower may leave the dealership with limited clarity about who owns the loan, when the account will be available, where the first payment should be sent, or how to enroll in automatic payment. Funding delays, booking delays, and a late welcome packet can create an apparent EPD that is partly an onboarding failure.

The welcome process should be treated as an early-payment control. The credit union should send the welcome packet promptly after booking with the account number, first-payment due date and amount, payment channels, automatic-payment instructions, and a reliable contact point. A welcome call, message, or approved electronic communication can reinforce that information and surface confusion before the due date. Management should track whether the communication was sent and whether delayed booking left too little time for the borrower to act.

Chapter 4 covers the payment channels themselves. A welcome packet that names a method the credit union cannot yet accept, or an account that is not payable for several days after booking, is an onboarding failure rather than a borrower one, and it should be ruled out before an early payment default is attributed to the dealer.

When an EPD occurs, management should distinguish among borrower hardship, fraud or misrepresentation, underwriting weakness, dealer conduct, and credit-union onboarding failure. That distinction determines whether the response belongs with collections, underwriting, the dealer, funding operations, or member onboarding.

Case Study: The Dealer With Only Three Bad Loans

A dealer produces 120 funded loans in its first year. Delinquency appears acceptable and only three loans become early payment defaults.

Management initially treats the three loans as isolated. Further review finds that all three applications used the same F&I employee, each showed income substantially above available estimates, and two contained address inconsistencies corrected after approval.

The review also confirms that welcome packets were sent promptly and the borrowers had usable payment instructions, allowing management to focus on the repeated application pattern rather than a servicing handoff problem.

The credit union places the dealer under enhanced review and monitors whether the pattern continues.

> **Lesson:** A small number can still be a strong signal when the underlying facts repeat.

Moving Dealer Risk Ratings Up or Down

An initial dealer risk rating gets assigned at onboarding; what follows is how that rating should change once real performance exists.

The scorecard's own output and the dealer's account-level risk rating are related but not identical. The companion tool produces a suggested rating of standard, watch, or restricted based on the composite risk index, or immediate review when a hard trigger fires. The account-level dealer risk rating is the broader classification management actually assigns to the relationship, and it includes two states the scorecard itself cannot produce, suspended and removed, because those are account actions a person takes, not a number a spreadsheet calculates.

The rating should reflect current evidence rather than historical reputation. A dealer that began under elevated review should be able to earn normal treatment. A long-standing dealer should be able to move downward when performance deteriorates.

A simple structure may be more useful than a complicated one:

- Standard: performance remains within expectations and no material concerns are unresolved.
- Watch: one or more measures show deterioration requiring increased review.
- Restricted: the dealer remains active under reduced limits, manual review, or other controls.
- Suspended: new business stops while management investigates or requires correction.
- Removed: the dealer is no longer included in the credit union's approved network.

Movement should be documented. The record should identify the evidence considered, the decision maker, the controls added or removed, the review period, and the conditions required for the next change.

KEY PRINCIPLE

Dealer ratings should move when the evidence moves. A permanent rating is not monitoring.

Corrective Action Plans

Monitoring has limited value if it only identifies problems. A scorecard that identifies a problem but never triggers corrective action is reporting, not risk management. Most dealer relationships do not move directly from satisfactory performance to suspension. More often, management identifies a trend, documents the concern, establishes expectations, and measures whether the dealer responds.

A corrective action plan provides structure for that middle step. It should be used when performance has deteriorated enough to require attention but remains potentially correctable. The objective is to determine whether the problem is understood, temporary, and capable of correction.

A corrective action plan should identify:

- The specific issue and supporting data.
- The improvement expected.
- The measurement period and interim review dates.
- The responsible dealer and credit union contacts.
- Temporary restrictions or enhanced review.
- The consequence if improvement does not occur.

Expectations should be measurable. "Improve documentation quality" is weak. "Reduce preventable funding defects below the defined threshold and eliminate aged title exceptions" is actionable. The threshold belongs in the scorecard or procedure, not in the chapter.

Corrective plans should close only after the measured problem improves and remains improved through a follow-up period. Completed activities are not the same as changed performance.

Case Study: The Plan That Closed on Time but Solved Nothing

The DRM clearly communicates a 90-day corrective action plan after repeated funding defects. The dealer acknowledges the issue, designates a new contact, and submits every requested response before the deadline.

Management closes the plan as completed. During the next quarter, the same defects return because the dealer never changed the underlying process.

The credit union changes the closure standard. Corrective plans now require evidence that the measured problem improved and remained improved.

> **Lesson:** Corrective action is measured by changed performance, not dealer acknowledgement.

Static Pools and Vintage Analysis

Dealer scorecards show differences across relationships. Static-pool and vintage analysis show differences across time.

A static pool groups loans originated during the same period and tracks how that group performs as it ages. Comparing vintages helps management see whether changes in dealers, underwriting, pricing, vehicle mix, or economic conditions improved or weakened the portfolio.

The practice should be standing, not assembled only for an examination. Management should compare origination periods at consistent ages. A one-year-old vintage should be compared with prior vintages when they were one year old, not with a fully matured portfolio.

Analysis can be performed for the program overall and segmented where volume permits by dealer, dealer group, credit tier, exception status, vehicle type, score band, or decision source.

Small programs should avoid false precision. The value comes from combining the trend with file review and operational context.

Several lending analytics platforms can build this kind of vintage comparison automatically rather than requiring a manual rebuild every quarter. Most of the major loan origination and core providers offer some version of it, either as a module or through a reporting partner, and several standalone analytics vendors serve the credit union market directly. Whether a purchased tool is worth adding depends on cost, existing system relationships, and whether the credit union's volume justifies it, but a small program does not need to build this analysis by hand if a tool it already has, or could reasonably add, already does it.

Use Aggregator Reporting, Then Fill the Gaps

The same informed-reliance principle that governs onboarding applies to monitoring. Management should use reporting already available through the network before building duplicate processes.

Management should inventory what its platform and LOS provide, how long the data is retained, whether reporting is available by dealer group, and whether information can be exported for internal analysis.

The credit union will still need information the aggregator may not hold, including loan performance after booking, complaints received directly, collection outcomes, internal exceptions, title aging, charge-offs, member-welcome timing, and corrective-action history. The final scorecard will likely combine platform, LOS, core, collections, complaint, and manual management data.

> KEY PRINCIPLE
> **Use the reports you already paid for. Build only what the existing systems do not provide.**

Portfolio Concentration Drift

Concentration limits get set at the policy level and tested again at each dealer's inclusion; what matters here is whether the portfolio stayed inside those limits after normal growth.

Concentration can develop without a new approval. One dealer may grow while others shrink. Several stores may be acquired by one ownership group. A manufacturer or region may become dominant even though no single onboarding decision appeared problematic.

Management should monitor concentration by outstanding balance and recent production, not only dealer count. Useful views include dealer, ownership group, manufacturer, geography, credit tier, vehicle type, and aggregator channel.

Individual rooftop scorecards are not enough when stores share ownership or operations. A dealer group may look acceptable store by store while common F&I turnover, title delays, complaint patterns, or corrective-action failures spread across the group. Management should review both the individual dealer and the combined ownership group, especially when personnel, systems, title processing, or product practices are shared.

The earlier drift is visible, the more options management has. New volume can be capped, access narrowed, pricing changed, or expansion paused before the concentration becomes difficult to unwind.

Case Study: The Limit Nobody Crossed

A credit union sets an opening limit for every dealer. Two years later, no individual dealer has violated its limit.

One dealer group has nevertheless acquired two stores, doubled production at another, and become the source of nearly one-third of recent indirect funding. Other dealers declined during the same period.

No single approval caused the concentration. Normal growth and ownership changes created it.

Management begins reporting balances and recent production by ownership group and pauses further expansion.

> **Lesson:** Every concentration begins as a successful strategy. Drift accumulates through many individually acceptable decisions.

Is the Score Model Still Working?

Score-model selection, and the risk that an unusual model could produce adverse selection, was addressed earlier in this book. What closes the loop is asking whether the model continues to separate risk as expected.

Management does not need to become a model-development team to do this; periodic outcome testing is enough. Do higher score bands continue to outperform lower bands? Are approval rates or score distributions changing? Are exceptions concentrated around a cutoff? Does the same score band perform differently by bureau, dealer, vehicle type, or vintage?

If the model no longer produces the expected ordering of risk, management should investigate data mapping, version changes, population shifts, decision-rule interaction, and underwriting practices before changing policy.

The important control is refusing to assume that a model chosen years ago still behaves the same way today.

Dealer Incentives, Awards, and the Trophy Case

Dealer incentives require the same discipline as employee incentives: management should understand what behavior the program rewards.

A dealer award may recognize volume, penetration, approval count, growth, speed, or another production measure. None of those outcomes is automatically bad. None is evidence of quality by itself.

An award should prompt a review. What behavior earned it? Did the same period also show higher exceptions, concentration, ancillary products, EPDs, complaints, title problems, or early payoffs? Did employees change decisions or responsiveness to preserve favored status?

The same applies to incentives the credit union pays dealers. A program may increase funded volume while also encouraging transactions that create more rework, weaker collateral, or poorer member outcomes.

The trophy case does not prove misconduct, but it is a reason to understand what the relationship has been optimized to produce.

> **KEY PRINCIPLE**
>
> **If someone gives the lending department a trophy, ask what behavior earned it.**

Case Study: The Trophy Nobody Examined

A dealer wins recognition for the highest indirect volume, the fastest growth, and the largest share of production in the credit union's network. Management celebrates the relationship at the next dealer appreciation event.

A routine scorecard review the same quarter tells a different story. Exception approvals at the dealer are rising, ancillary-product concentration is increasing, the dealer's share of the portfolio is drifting past what the group's concentration limits assumed, and early payment defaults are worsening.

None of these trends had been disqualifying on their own. Together, they show a relationship that was optimized for production while credit quality, operational quality, and concentration exposure moved in the wrong direction underneath it.

Management does not rescind the recognition, but it does open a corrective action review and resets the dealer's rating discussion for the next cycle based on the full scorecard, not the volume that earned the award.

> **Lesson:** Production awards measure production. They do not measure credit quality, operational quality, or member outcomes.

When Monitoring Leads to Restriction or Suspension

Not every weak score requires suspension. Not every serious event should wait for the next scorecard cycle.

Restriction may be appropriate when the relationship remains usable but requires lower volume, manual underwriting, enhanced documentation, title-before-funding, limited products, or more frequent review.

Suspension may be appropriate when continuing new business could deepen exposure while management investigates fraud, identity, systemic documentation, unresolved consumer harm, or failure to cooperate.

The decision should consider related stores when ownership, personnel, systems, or processes are shared. Chapter 7 established the removal process. Chapter 8 supplies the evidence that activates it.

Management should document why the response was proportionate, who approved it, what happens to pending applications, and what conditions would allow reinstatement.

Things That Get Credit Unions Into Trouble

Monitoring failures are rarely about missing data. They look like these:

- Using scorecards as reports without linking results to decisions.
- Allowing production to conceal weak credit or operational performance.
- Treating EPDs only as collection events instead of investigating dealer patterns.
- Assuming every apparent first-payment default is a borrower or dealer problem without checking booking delays, welcome timing, and payment instructions.
- Leaving dealer risk ratings unchanged after performance changes.
- Creating corrective plans with vague expectations or no follow-up measurement.
- Waiting for the next quarterly cycle to look at a trend that a hard escalation trigger should have surfaced immediately.
- Producing static-pool analysis only when an examiner asks.
- Rebuilding aggregator reports without understanding what is already available.
- Monitoring concentration at the rooftop but not the ownership-group level.
- Assuming a score model still works because it worked when selected.
- Treating awards, incentives, or high production as proof of dealer quality.
- Allowing familiarity to delay restriction or suspension.

The final governance failure is not a lack of data. Most programs have more data than management uses. The failure is allowing signals to accumulate without changing the relationship.

Chapter Summary

- Dealer monitoring should determine whether a relationship is improving, stable, or deteriorating and identify the response that follows.
- Eight core measures across credit performance, operational quality, production and conversion, and member impact and relationship are enough to govern a small program well. More measures usually just make the scorecard harder to keep current.
- Review cadence should be simple enough to sustain: monthly for a new dealer's first three months, quarterly for every measure and every dealer after that.
- Responsiveness and cooperation matter and belong in the corrective action and rating discussion directly. They are judgment calls, not a separate scored category competing for space on the scorecard.
- A composite score organizes judgment but should not erase a serious control failure. Any of the three hard escalation triggers should override the score and produce a suggested rating of immediate review.

- EPDs should be reviewed by dealer, F&I employee where available, underwriter, credit tier, and cause, including whether delayed booking or weak welcome communications contributed.
- Dealer risk ratings should move when performance moves.
- Corrective action plans should define measurable improvement and close only after performance changes.
- Static-pool and vintage analysis should be a standing practice.
- Management should use aggregator reporting and combine it with internal loan, complaint, title, exception, collection, and welcome-process data.
- Concentration should be monitored by balance and recent production, including shared operating problems across dealer groups.
- Score models should be tested periodically against outcomes.
- Awards and incentives should prompt review of the behavior being rewarded.
- Restriction and suspension are management tools, not admissions that onboarding failed.

Board Discussion Questions

1. Do the eight core scorecard measures and their weighting prevent production from masking weak credit or operational quality?
2. Is our review cadence for each measure something management can actually sustain

quarter after quarter, or does it look thorough on paper but lapse in practice?

3. What conditions trigger immediate review regardless of the overall score?
4. How are EPDs connected back to dealers, F&I staff, underwriters, application data, booking timeliness, and the member welcome process?
5. What moves a dealer from standard to watch, restricted, suspended, or removed?
6. Who approves rating changes and confirms related controls were implemented?
7. What makes a corrective action plan successful, and who confirms improvement was sustained?
8. How does management compare vintages at consistent ages?
9. What reports already exist through the aggregator, and what gaps remain?
10. How does management identify concentration and shared operating problems across dealer groups?
11. What evidence shows score models and decision rules continue to separate risk as expected?
12. What incentives could reward volume while weakening quality?
13. When would management restrict or suspend a profitable dealer?

CEO Action Items

1. Finalize the eight core scorecard measures, their thresholds and weighting, and a review cadence the team can sustain, using Appendix A as the starting framework.
2. Assign responsibility for combining aggregator, LOS, core, collections, title, complaint, welcome-process, and management data.
3. Create an EPD review process that distinguishes credit or fraud concerns from booking and welcome-process failures.
4. Define dealer risk-rating categories, movement criteria, approving authority, and required controls.
5. Create a corrective action plan template with measurable expectations, interim reviews, consequences, and post-closure validation.
6. Establish standing static-pool and vintage reporting at consistent loan ages.
7. Inventory reports available from the aggregator and identify which measures must be built internally.
8. Monitor concentration by dealer, ownership group, geography, manufacturer, credit tier, and recent production, including shared F&I, title, complaint, and corrective-action trends.
9. Establish a proportionate process for testing score-band and decision-rule performance.
10. Review dealer and employee incentives for the behavior they reward.

11. Define restriction, suspension, reinstatement, and removal authority before the first serious event occurs.
12. Ensure board reporting highlights decisions and emerging risks rather than every dealer-level metric.

Appendix A: Dealer Scorecard Blueprint

This is the structural framework for evaluating dealer performance. A companion workbook, the Dealer Scorecard Tool, contains the working version of this framework: entry fields for each measure, illustrative risk thresholds and category weights, and a formula-driven composite risk index and suggested rating. Each measure converts to a 1 (low risk), 2 (medium risk), or 3 (high risk) score. The four category averages combine into a single composite risk index from 1.00 to 3.00, mapped to a suggested rating of standard, watch, or restricted, unless a hard trigger overrides it to immediate review. The thresholds in that workbook are a starting point. Each credit union should calibrate them to its own portfolio, systems, and risk appetite before relying on the output.

What follows is the illustrative governance framework behind that tool.

Category & Weight	Core Measures	Warning Signs (Risk Score Rises)
Credit Performance **35%**	Delinquency (60+ days) Early Payment Defaults (EPDs) Early Payoffs	EPDs clustering around specific F&I staff; delinquency trending up quarter over quarter; early payoffs rising sharply.
Operational Quality **30%**	Title Aging (>60 Days) Loan Package Quality: rate of major defects requiring a contract to be re-signed (approved amount exceeded, incorrect rate or term, or a major structural error)	Titles extending past 60 days on more than an isolated loan; a rising rate of packages requiring re-signing for a major defect, not routine missing initials.
Production & Conversion **15%**	Funded Loan Volume vs. expectations Look-to-Book Ratio	Volume or look-to-book drifting well outside the range the credit union expected from the relationship.
Member Impact & Relationship **20%**	Substantiated Member Complaints (attributed to the dealer or transaction)	Repeated complaints of the same type; complaints tied to misrepresentation, discouragement, or unresolved refunds.

Review cadence is simple and uniform: monthly for a new dealer's first three months, quarterly for every measure and every dealer after that.

HARD ESCALATION TRIGGERS

A failure in any of the following categories overrides the composite risk index and returns a suggested rating of immediate review, regardless of how favorable the score otherwise looks:

- **Confirmed Fraud:** Evidence of synthetic identity, power booking, altered income documents, or similar intentional misconduct.
- **Compliance or Legal Failure:** A material pattern involving fair-lending concerns, Holder Rule-related dealer conduct, or origination outside approved geographic boundaries.
- **Failure to Cure:** The dealer refuses to complete a formal corrective action plan, cooperate with investigation, or honor a valid repurchase or reimbursement obligation.

HOW TO USE THE BLUEPRINT

- Review performance at both the rooftop and ownership-group levels.
- Apply the same metric definitions consistently across dealers.
- Use production as context, not as compensation for weak quality.
- Investigate metric changes before automatically changing a rating.

- Document rating decisions, restrictions, corrective plans, and reinstatement conditions.
- Revisit weights and thresholds after enough performance history exists to test whether the scorecard distinguishes risk as intended.

Final Summary: Discipline Is the Strategy

Indirect auto lending is not a shortcut to loan growth. It is a disciplined operating choice. The central lesson of this book is simple: volume is not a strategy. Volume is an outcome, and sometimes a misleading one. The strategy is the set of boundaries that determines which volume the credit union will accept, which dealer relationships it will build, and which risks it will refuse.

A sound program begins before the first application arrives. The board must define risk appetite, concentration limits, credit-tier boundaries, dealer-type boundaries, exception authority, and the reporting needed to see whether the program remains inside those choices. Management must then turn that intent into daily operating discipline: underwriting rules, technology configuration, staffing coverage, dealer communication, documentation, compliance testing, and ongoing monitoring.

For a small or newly entering credit union, the safest starting point remains narrow by design: prime and super-prime borrowers, franchise dealers as the default, clear limits on exceptions and concentration, and reporting that reaches below delinquency. No program avoids risk entirely. The goal is to choose risks the institution understands, can price, can monitor, and can explain when conditions change.

Before building, expanding, or resetting an indirect program, leadership should be able to answer five questions plainly:

- Do we know why we are in this channel?
- Do we know which borrowers and dealers fit our strategy?
- Can our systems, people, policies, and vendors execute the standards we approved?
- Can we see risk building before losses appear?
- Are we prepared to slow, restrict, or end volume that does not fit?

If the answer is yes, indirect lending can be a useful and responsible part of the credit union's lending strategy. If the answer is no, more volume will not solve the weakness. It will enlarge it.

A credit union does not need to be the biggest lender on the platform, approve the most applications, or maintain the broadest dealer network. It needs to know what it is trying to do, build the controls to do it consistently, and retain the courage to say no when the next loan, dealer, or growth target would pull the program outside those controls.

Indirect lending can produce growth, yield, and market presence. But only discipline can make those outcomes durable. Volume is never the strategy. Discipline is.

Glossary of Terms

Every term defined in the book, in one place. The chapter reference points to where the term is introduced and discussed.

A

Adverse Action Notice: A notice required under ECOA and Regulation B informing an applicant of a qualifying adverse credit decision and the principal reasons for that decision. (Ch. 5)

Adverse Selection: The tendency of a lending standard to attract the applicants it was least intended to serve, as when a documentation requirement drives away borrowers who have other options and retains those who do not. (Ch. 4)

Aggregator: A platform such as CUDL, RouteOne, or Dealertrack that routes a dealer's financing application to multiple lenders simultaneously. (Ch. 1)

ALCO (Asset Liability Committee): The internal committee responsible for managing a credit union's interest rate risk and balance sheet composition. (Ch. 1)

Approved Dealer Network: The group of dealers authorized to submit applications to the credit union through the indirect program. (Ch. 2)

Auto-Enhanced Credit Score: A credit score model built specifically to predict how a borrower will perform on an auto loan, rather than a general-purpose score built to predict credit risk broadly. (Ch. 4)

Automated Decision Rules: System-configured underwriting criteria that produce an approval, decline, or referral based on defined standards. (Ch. 3)

B

Business Continuity (Technology): The plan for maintaining lending operations through a vendor outage, system failure, or loss of access to a data source such as a credit bureau. (Ch. 4)

Buy Rate: The interest rate a lender is willing to offer a specific borrower before any dealer markup is added. (Ch. 5)

C

Capacity Discipline: Ensuring loan volume does not exceed the credit union's underwriting, processing, funding, liquidity, and servicing capacity. (Ch. 2)

Chargeback: Recovery of a defined fee, refund, loss, or other amount associated with a dealer transaction. (Ch. 7)

Compensating Factor: A documented strength that may mitigate a specific weakness or exception in an application. (Ch. 3)

Concentration Drift: Growth in exposure to a dealer, ownership group, geography, manufacturer, or other segment after initial limits were established. (Ch. 8)

Corrective Action Plan: A documented set of measurable actions and review dates intended to correct dealer-performance problems before stronger restrictions are required. (Ch. 8)

CUSO (Credit Union Service Organization): An entity owned by one or more credit unions that can provide services, including indirect lending support, on their behalf. (Ch. 4)

D

Dealer Coaching: Providing information that goes beyond explaining standards and enables a dealer to structure or present transactions around internal controls. (Ch. 6)

Dealer Group Concentration: Exposure created by multiple stores sharing ownership, management, F&I practices, title operations, vendors, or other dependencies. (Ch. 7)

Dealer Markup: An amount added by a dealer above a lender's buy rate or other compensation associated with arranging financing. (Ch. 5)

Dealer Relationship Manager (DRM): The employee responsible for managing communication and business relationships with approved dealers without independently owning credit decisions unless separately authorized. (Ch. 6)

Dealer Reserve: The compensation a dealer earns for arranging financing through a lender, typically structured as a flat fee or a capped markup over the lender's buy rate. (Ch. 2)

Dealer Risk Rating: The current management classification determining review, limits, or restrictions applied to a dealer. (Ch. 8)

Dealer Scorecard: A structured evaluation weighting four categories (credit performance, operational quality, production and conversion, and member impact and relationship) into a single composite risk index to support dealer decisions. (Ch. 8)

Dealer Submission Platform: A system, separate from the lender's loan origination system, that a dealer uses to submit an application and select among competing lenders. (Ch. 4)

Debt-to-Income (DTI): A ratio comparing a borrower's monthly debt obligations to income, used as a supplementary indicator of repayment capacity alongside a credit score. (Ch. 4)

Decision Authority: The formally assigned power to approve, decline, override, waive, or escalate a lending or dealer-management decision. (Ch. 6)

Decision Engine: The system component that applies automated underwriting rules to an application and produces an approval, decline, or referral. (Ch. 4)

E

Early Payoff: A loan paid off materially earlier than expected, which may reduce program value and indicate refinancing, pricing, or dealer-fit issues. (Ch. 8)

EPD (Early Payment Default): A loan that becomes seriously delinquent or defaults within a short window after funding, often used as a leading indicator of underwriting weakness, fraud, or a failure in the credit union's own onboarding process. Chapter 8 develops this as a dealer-level measure. (Ch. 1)

Exception Band: The defined range within which management may approve deviations from standard underwriting requirements. (Ch. 6)

F

Fair Lending Review: An analysis of lending outcomes and processes intended to identify potentially inconsistent treatment or unexplained disparities. (Ch. 5)

F&I (Finance and Insurance): The dealership department that arranges financing and sells related products like GAP and extended warranties at the point of sale. (Ch. 2)

Final Decision Time: The time from application receipt until the transaction has reached a usable final outcome, including resolution of referrals, stipulations, and necessary conditions. (Ch. 6)

G

Geographic Discipline: Limiting dealer access and borrower reach to markets the credit union can reasonably serve, monitor, and support. (Ch. 2)

Go/No-Go Decision: The formal decision to proceed, pause, narrow, or decline an indirect lending program based on feasibility findings. (Ch. 2)

H

Hard Escalation Trigger: A condition that overrides the composite risk index and returns a suggested rating of immediate review regardless of the dealer's underlying score. Appendix A defines the three triggers. (Ch. 8)

Hard Knockout: A condition that stops a transaction under the decision rules and generally provides no routine override path. (Ch. 3)

Holder Rule: The FTC's Trade Regulation Rule Concerning Preservation of Consumers' Claims and Defenses (16 CFR Part 433), which subjects the holder of a consumer credit contract to the same claims and defenses the buyer could raise against the original seller. (Ch. 1)

I

Income-Estimation Score: A score or estimate, derived from credit bureau and other data sources, used to approximate a borrower's income when direct verification is not obtained. (Ch. 4)

Initial Dealer Risk Rating: The onboarding classification that determines how cautiously a dealer relationship begins before the credit union has enough performance history for ongoing monitoring. (Ch. 7)

K

Key-Person Risk: Operational risk created when critical knowledge, authority, relationships, or processes depend on one individual. (Ch. 6)

L

Lender of Last Resort: A lender that becomes known primarily as a place to send difficult or previously declined applications rather than as a valued relationship partner. (Ch. 2)

Loan Origination System (LOS): The lender's internal system of record for underwriting, documentation, funding, and compliance on a loan. (Ch. 4)

Look-to-Book Ratio: The relationship between applications received and loans funded, used to understand conversion and dealer fit. (Ch. 8)

M

Market Feasibility: The process of determining whether an indirect lending opportunity realistically exists in the credit union's market and can be pursued within its risk appetite and capacity. (Ch. 2)

P

Payment Channel: The method by which a borrower remits a loan payment, including recurring ACH from an external account, one-time ACH, debit card, agent-assisted payment, or mailed check. (Ch. 4)

Policy Drift: The gradual movement away from approved standards through repeated exceptions, informal practices, or undocumented changes. (Ch. 3)

Power Booking: Dealer fraud involving misrepresentation of a vehicle's condition, mileage, equipment, or history to inflate its financed value. (Ch. 1)

Pricing Exception: A documented deviation from standard pricing or compensation terms. (Ch. 5)

Progressive Authority: A training approach in which an employee receives broader decision authority after demonstrating proficiency and consistent judgment. (Ch. 6)

Q

R

Recourse: A contractual right to recover specified losses or amounts when defined conditions occur. (Ch. 7)

Repurchase: A remedy requiring a dealer to buy back a contract when a qualifying trigger is met. (Ch. 7)

RISA: A state retail installment sales act governing aspects of retail installment contracts and vehicle finance. (Ch. 5)

Risk-Free Benchmark: A reference rate, such as the two-year Treasury yield, representing the return available on a similar-duration investment carrying no credit risk, used as the floor for building a loan rate. (Ch. 2)

S

Second Look: A reconsideration of an initial decision after corrected data, additional information, or a restructured transaction is provided. (Ch. 3)

Service-Level Agreement (SLA): A vendor's contractual commitment regarding system uptime, support responsiveness, and issue resolution timelines. (Ch. 4)

Static Pool Analysis: A method of tracking the performance of a group of loans originated in the same period, used to measure life-of-loan loss expectations for an indirect program. (Ch. 1)

Stipulation: A condition attached to an approval that must be satisfied before funding, such as proof of income, residence, or insurance. (Ch. 3)

T

Technical Activation: The system or platform action that allows a dealer to submit applications to the credit union. (Ch. 7)

Technology Debt: The accumulated cost of manual workarounds, informal tools, and deferred system fixes that were never formally replaced with a governed solution. (Ch. 4)

Title Aging Report: A report tracking funded loans for which evidence of correct lien perfection has not been received within expected timeframes. (Ch. 4)

Transaction Quality: The overall reasonableness of the transaction structure, including collateral exposure, reputation risk, and member-treatment considerations, not merely repayment probability. (Ch. 3)

U

UDAAP: Unfair, deceptive, or abusive acts or practices that may create consumer harm and regulatory, legal, or reputation risk. (Ch. 5)

V

Verification of Income (VOI): Direct documentation of a borrower's income, such as pay stubs, W-2s, or tax returns, as distinguished from an income-estimation score derived from bureau and other data. (Ch. 1)

Vintage Analysis: Comparison of loan groups from different origination periods at comparable ages. (Ch. 8)

W

Weighted Average Life: The average time a dollar of principal remains outstanding on a loan or pool of loans, accounting for scheduled payments and prepayments, used to match a loan's duration to an appropriate benchmark rate. (Ch. 2)

About the Author

Jeff Bassill has spent 45 years in banking and credit unions, including four decades in indirect auto lending and credit risk management. Over that career he has led retail operations, underwriting, compliance, and loss mitigation for financial institutions across Central California.

Jeff served as President and Chief Executive Officer of Kings Federal Credit Union for eight years before moving into his current semi-retired role as Chief Financial and Risk Officer. Earlier he was Executive Vice President and Chief Operating Officer at Noble Credit Union, formerly Fresno County Federal Credit Union, where he oversaw retail lending and operations across seven branches. He also spent nine years in branch leadership at Bank of the West.

Alongside his executive work, Jeff spent more than six years as Certified Core Adjunct Faculty at National University's School of Business, teaching corporate finance, real estate finance, and risk management. He is the founder of CU Risk Advisors (https://mycurisk.com) and the creator of ExpressHold, a web-based compliance tool that streamlines Regulation CC check holds for community financial institutions.

Jeff holds an MBA from Colorado State University and is a graduate of the Pacific Coast Banking School at the University of Washington.

Jeff can be reached at jeff@mycurisk.com.

www.ingramcontent.com/pod-product-compliance
Lightning Source LLC
LaVergne TN
LVHW010716061126
851857LV00014B/1219
9798997833107